The Classic Book of Dirty Jokes

The Classic Book of Dirty Jokes

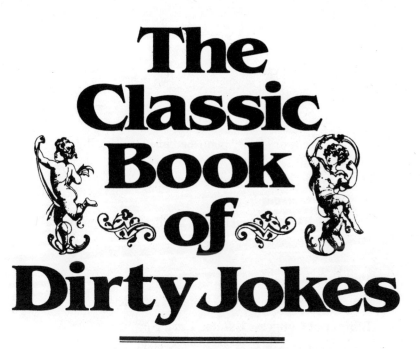

FORMERLY ENTITLED
Anecdota Americana

With a New Foreword by
Al Goldstein

Bell Publishing Company

New York

This book was originally published in 1928, in a slightly different form, as *Anecdota Americana*.

Copyright © 1981 by Crown Publishers, Inc.
All rights reserved.

This edition is published by Bell Publishing Company.

1981 EDITION

Manufactured in the United States of America

Library of Congress Catalog Card Number: 81-4835

ISBN: 0-517-336367

g h

FOREWORD

THE year was 1928; money was easy, Art Deco glittered, cars were exotic and libidos were breaking out. Flappers were picked up in Duesenbergs and Packards by young men with pocket flasks.

Johnny Weismuller established a new world record for the 100-meter freestyle, and Ty Cobb retired. It was the age of glittering youth: lay science circles were abuzz with the possibility of rejuvenation through gland transplants.

Life was gay and secure; the stock market was soaring, and sixty-two nations had signed the Kellogg-Briand Treaty which renounced war "as an instrument of national policy." Bessie Smith sang "Poor Man's Blues" to rich men's sons. Al Jolson's "Sonnyboy" sold twelve million in its first four weeks. Bands played "Makin' Whoopee" and crooners sang, "I Can't Give You Anything But Love."

Walt Disney released his first Mickey Mouse cartoon, *Plane Crazy* and followed it up with the classic *Steamboat Willie*, starring Mickey playing "Farmer in the Dell" on the udders of a cow.

And, in 1928, amidst the gaiety and ribaldry, a jewel appeared, the *Anecdota Americana*, a compilation of very American, very raucous humor. This book is regarded by many as the original "dirty joke" book and it is not only outrageous and funny, but often brilliantly mirrors our sexual inversions, hypocrisies and befuddlements.

Most of us deal with the incomprehensibilities of our

lives by laughing. It is a method of self-defense, a way of exorcising devils. Humor is a means of conquering the unfathomable and accepting it. People who can't laugh at a good dirty joke are not ready to face the complexities of their own sexual natures ... they say that adolescent males most enjoy a dirty joke, and for them, who are more in touch with their own often overwhelming sexuality, laughter is a safety valve. Laughter at our sexual natures is laughter at ourselves, at our pomposity, our insistence on our own importance in this universe. Laughter puts us in our place and gives us a moment to stand back and get ourselves and our society in perspective.

The Dinktown band was doing its best when someone called the piccolo player a cock-sucker. The band leader's baton beat a tattoo on his music stand and the players became silent. "Who called my piccolo player a cock-sucker?" he demanded. A voice from the rear of the theatre yelled back, "Who called that cock-sucker a piccolo player?"

We laugh, and for a moment we realize dirty words are just a form of expression, we have defused the social taboos, and we stand on firm ground.

This book contains many entertaining opportunities to laugh, and by doing so, engage in a great human activity.

AL GOLDSTEIN

ANECDOTES COLLECTED AND TAKEN DOWN BY
℗   ℗   ℗   *Mr. William Passemon*
PEN AND INK DRAWINGS BY *Anton Erdman*
WOOD-BLOCKS DRAWN & CUT BY *Bruce MacAile*

DEDICATION

To all those who
by their efforts, passive and active,
have made possible this book, these,
the ripest fruits of their labors ❧

GENTLEMEN: IN THE EVENT YOU
do not clearly understand the neat
abstraction of our dedication, we take
the pains candidly to inform you
that this book is inscribed to all
prudes, puritans, hypocrites,
censors, and moralists,
that have ever been, are, or shall be.

The Classic Book of Dirty Jokes

aboard," the conductor called down the platform. And the train had no sooner started than a slim Englishman entered the smoking compartment of the pullman. ❡ "Gentlemen," he said to the men that crowded the room, "is there any reason why we shouldn't begin to talk cunt right away?"

2

IN THE corner seat a playwright braced himself to listen complacently. That which ran through his mind was,

"Hush little sex-joke, don't you cry,
You'll be a drama bye and bye."

3

"I DON'T tell dirty stories," came a high voice from a little man. "I like to listen, but I don't tell them. I can't remember the darn things."

4

A N ENGLISHMAN entered a drug store and went to the back counter. "Show me some condoms," he said to the clerk. "What kind, the twenty-five cent ones or the fifties?" asked the clerk. "Well, I say, what's the difference?" asked the limey. "The fifty-cent ones you can wash, and use again and again," he was informed. "Fine," he said, "what an economy, I'll take several." ⟨ In a few weeks he returned to the drug store, went up to the clerk and said: "You may sell me several condoms, but *not* the fifty-cent ones, that *wash*." "Why not, what's the matter?" the clerk asked. "Didn't they work all right?" "I suppose they did," retorted the Englishman, "but I got a nasty note from my laundry.

5

A NOTHER drug store story recounts the experience of a large Westerner, who, troubled by a horny feeling which he had no immediate prospect of relieving, went to a pharmacist to get something for it in the way of a bromide. He was somewhat embarrassed when he found a woman in attendance. "Pardon me," he said, "but I'd like to see the boss." "Why, I'm the boss," said the woman. "Well then, a-er, man clerk," said the Westerner. "We haven't any," the owner replied, "you can tell me what you want. I won't be embarrassed." ⟨ "Well," said the stranger, "I've got an awful hard on. What can you give me for it?" ⟨ "Just a minute," said the woman, and went to the back of the drug store. In a few minutes she returned.

"I've just been talking it over with my sister, who makes up the prescriptions, and who is my partner in this store," she said, "and the best we can give you is the store and two hundred dollars."

6

A SMALL boy entered a drug store and whispered to the clerk that he wanted some condoms. "What size," he was asked, "and who are they for?" "Gimme assorted sizes," he said, "they're for my sister, she's goin' to the country."

7

IN A certain drug store on the upper west side a man entered one day, and seeing only a woman in attendance asked for the proprietor, or a male clerk. "I'm the proprietor, and we have no male clerk," she said; "tell me what you want." "Well," said the man, "I want a few condoms." "What size?" asked the woman. "I don't know. Do they come in sizes?" ❡ "Come back here," said the owner, taking him behind the partition to the rear of the store. "Put it in," she added, throwing herself on a couch and lifting her skirts. The customer readily complied, and as he inserted his prober the proprietor said, "Size 7, take it out. How many do you want?" ❡ In somewhat of a daze the customer left the place, and coming across Levy told him his adventure. Then Levy went immediately to the same store, where, pretending to be embarrassed he allowed himself to be coaxed into asking the woman for

condoms. He also affected great surprise to learn they came
in sizes, and when he was invited to the rear of the store
complied readily. "We'll soon find out what size you are,"
said the woman throwing herself again on the couch. "Put it
all the way in." Levy did as he was told, but neglected to
take it out until his sperm left him in one grand ejaculation.
"You take size 8," said the woman, rising, "how many do
you want." "I don't want any," said Levy, "I just came in
for a fitting."

8

O NE OF the oldest of drug store stories is the one
about the man who wanted some condoms and was
also invited to the rear of the store by the lady clerk,
to get the right size. ⁋ "Take it out," she said, and
when he did the lady took his penis in one hand while
with the other she attempted to measure it. "Size 3,"
she said, "no, 4, Mame, no, no, 7, Mamie, no, no, 8—
Mamie, bring the mop."

9

A SPIRITUALIST meeting was in progress. The leader
had just finished expounding his sermon, and he
called to his sweltering, panting audience: "We will now
have the personal part of the program. Is there any among
the brethren that has had some intercourse with ghosts?
This is the experience part of the meeting. Again, I ask, is
there any among the brethren that has had any intercourse
with a ghost? A small fellow in the rear of the auditorium

raised his hand. "I have," he said, in a small voice. Step this way, brother, step this way!" the leader shouted. Then as the little fellow approached the rostrum he called, "Now tell the brethren just what has been your intercourse with a ghost." "I beg your pardon," said the little man, "I thought you said 'goat.'"

10

COHN met Levy for the first time in years. ¶ "How is things, Levy?" he asked, "I hear you got very rich here in America." ¶ "I can't complain," the other replied. "I got a house and garden in the country, a ottomobile, a wife with ten children and money in the bank." ¶ Cohn, nettled, tried the soften the hurt of his friend's success. ¶ "Well," he said, "after all, in a day what can you do that I can't? We both eat, sleep and drink. What else is in a life." ¶ "Aaah," said Levy, "you call your life living? In the morning I get up, have a fine breakfast, followed by a good perfecto cigar. Then I lay on my verandah. After that I play a round golluf and come back with a healthy appetite for lunch. When I finish I have a fine perfecto cigar, lay on my verandah again, and am ready for an afternoon with my ottomobile. I come back for sopper with a appetite like a wolf. After sopper I smoke a good long cigar, lay on my verandah again, and at night go to the theatre, the opera, where I like." ¶ "That's wonderful! And you don't do no work?" said Cohen, marvelling. On his return home he told his wife of the encounter. ¶ "You know who I met today?" he announced. "Levy, what came over on the ship with me. Is that man rich! He's got a house and garden in the country, an ottemobile, a wife with ten children. . . ." ❡ Mrs. Cohen interrupted: "What's his wife's name?" ❡ "I don't know," said her husband, "but I think its 'verandah.' "

11

THE DINKTOWN band was doing its best when someone called the picollo player a cock-sucker. The leader's baton beat a tatoo on his music stand, and the players became silent. He turned to his audience. ❡ "Who called my picollo player a cock-sucker?" he demanded. ❡ A voice in the rear of the theatre yelled back: "Who called that cock-sucker a picollo player?"

12

EVERY Sunday morning when the auld folks had gone to the kirk Annie would be visited by her lover, Jock, and they would seize the service hours as opportune for screwing. One bright Sabbath day Jock arrived just after the auld folks had departed, and whistling a bonnie air leaped up the steps three at a time to Annie's bedroom. The lass was removing her waist when Jock burst in, puffing the final bars of *Annie Laurie*. His sweetheart gave him a disapproving look. ❡ Jock apparently didn't notice this, for, putting his arms around Annie he began another tune. The lass tore herself from his arms and began to redress. ❡ "Why, what is it, Annie?" asked Jock. "Have I done aught to offend ye?" ❡ "Stop it, stop it," said

the girl. "Ye were whistlin' an' I will no fornicate wi'
a man wha whistles on the Sabbath!"

13

THE HEIGHT of Ambition: A flea climbing up an
elephant's hind leg, with intent to commit rape!

14

THE HEIGHT of precaution: An old maid putting
a condom on her candle.

15

MOTHER had just finished her bath and stood in
the tub, drying herself. One foot rested on the
edge of the tub. Sonny stood near by, looking on.
"Ooh, mamma," he prattled, "who cut you?" pointing
to the gash God gave her. ¶ "Papa did that," said
the mother, in her sweetest tones. ¶ "Cut you right
near the cunt, didn't he," the child said.

16

THE LOCAL pastor was on trial before his flock, for
various misdeeds. During the proceedings, which
were of a solemn nature, he leered at his accusers and
snickered at their evidence. He was finally called upon to
say a few words in his defense. "Folks," he began, "you all
are accusing me of various nefarious crimes. You don't have

to prove 'em, I admit 'em. I have done everything you all said, and more. But I've been a good pastor to you, and now I'm going away. As I pass down the aisle, however, kindly take notice that I have placed a sprig of mistletoe just under my coattails."

17

Two young movie actresses from Hollywood met in the studio during the lunch rest period, and one complained to the other that she had been troubled for quite a time with crab lice. "How can I get rid of them?" she asked. ⁋ "Just rub in some Paris green," said her friend, "that'll kill 'em." ⁋ A week or so later on they again met, and the first girl asked the other: "Did you rub in that Paris green I told you?" ⁋ "Yes," said the afflicted one. ⁋ "Did it kill the crabs?" ⁋ "Yep, and a couple of directors too."

18

Sven got into the mine elevator, chuckling out loud. ⁋ "What's the joke, Sven?" asked the mine foreman. ⁋ "Ay bane have good yoke on Ole," the bohunk replied. "Ay just find out Ole pay my wife five dollars to foke her and I foke her for nothing."

19

Jones, troubled with a hoarse throat, so that his voice rose barely above a whisper, rushed to his doctor.

The doctor's pretty young wife answered the bell. "Is the doctor in?" Jones asked in husky tones. ⟨ "No, come in," the fair matron whispered back.

20

ON A lonely road, far from any town the traveller's car suddenly stopped dead. A quick examination showed him there was no gasoline left in the tank. Night had fallen and he made his way towards a light in a house some distance away. A knock on the door brought a beautiful woman in answer. ⟨ "Pardon me, madam," said the tourist, "but my car has broken down. I wonder if you couldn't put me up for the night here?" ⟨ "Well," said the lady, "I'm all alone, but I guess I'll take a chance." And she escorted him to a neat little room on the next floor. ⟨ As he prepared himself for bed the motorist couldn't help thinking how much more pleasant it would be if the young woman would come into bed with him. It would be a beastly way to repay her hospitality, he thought, to make any advances, but he could not keep from thinking of her beautiful form, neatly outlined in the flimsy wrapper she wore. Finally, with a sigh, he crawled into bed. But he could not sleep. He found himself still thinking of the fair and lonely lady. Gradually the sheets assumed the form of a tent above him. There was a sudden, soft tap at his door. ⟨ "Come in," he shouted, glee in his voice. A smiling face showed itself in the doorway, a golden, smiling, warm, inviting countenance. ⟨ "Would you like company?" the young lady said, sweetly, softly. ⟨ "Would I?" the guest shouted, "You just bet your life I would." ⟨ "That's fine," the lady replied. "You see another gentleman whose car broke down is at the door and wants me to put him up!"

2 1

Sammy, lately of Jersey, was in the trenches with his buddies, hard at the business of winning the war. For five days there had been no lull in the fighting. The men had had very little sleep, cut off as they were from the main body, and there was much speculation as to when a relief unit could come up. Sammy didn't particularly care whether he were shot or lived. It isn't particularly cheerful to be several thousand miles from home, without a letter to connect you with dear ones left behind. And Sammy hadn't heard from his wife in months. Suddenly he noticed next to him a strange man. And then all about him he saw others of a different regiment. Relief had come at last. For an hour or more the fighting continued with even greater ferocity, and then, suddenly there came a lull. Sammy threw himself to the ground, near the stranger he had first noticed. There was some conversation, cut short when a package of letters was thrust into Sammy's hands. His eyes showed joy. Eagerly he tore open the first of the fat letters and devoured the writing, the strange man meanwhile looking on casually. Suddenly Sammy held his hand up to the light. "See that, boy?" he said. "If that isn't the most considerate wife. Look at that; she sent me hair right off her snatch. Hot dog!" The other fellow reached over, took the hair from Sammy, ran it delicately through his fingers, gazed at it in the sunlight, then turned to Sammy, "Pardon me," he said, "but isn't your name Hawkins?"

22

CLITO: King Solomon had a thousand wives, they say . How could he tell which one to screw?

23

THERE was a lull in the firing of the big guns and a young soldier named Lincoln Smith spied a cow meandering aimlessly across a field. He turned to his friend Hamilton Burr and said, with considerable fervor: "Oh, boy, see that? Oh, if it was only a woman." Alexander turned back to him and said with equal fervor: "Oh, boy, if it was only dark."

24

A New Yorker once boasted that a friend of his was endowed with a wondrous sense of smell. Just one sniff at an object, in the dark, and he could tell what it was. So it was decided that his powers be put to the test and an assortment of twigs was brought to a room, in which was the wizard, blindfolded. ⟨ One of the twigs was held under his nose for an instant. "Pine," said the man with the keen sense of smell. Another twig he guessed to be birch, another oak, another hickory and so on, all correctly. One of the invited company, further to test the powers of this gifted nose, then held under it his middle finger, which had just come from an exploration of a maid's private parts. ⟨ "Hollywood," the wizard guessed.

25

RANDALL JOHNSON took his sweetie out for a buggy ride. As they got out into the country he pulled in the reins. "Whoa," he said. Then turning to the girl, "how about a little piece, Mary? "Uh-uh," said the girl, "I can't. I'm ill." "Giddap," said Randy. A little further into the country, in an even more secluded spot he reined in again. "Whoa," he said, "Mary, it's a little more lonely here. You got another way to satisfy me?" "Uh-uh," said Mary, "can't do anything here. I've got piles." "Giddap," said Johnson. As they drove, they got further into the woods, and Randy turned into a side road. "Whoa," he yelled, and leaping from the buggy he picked up a large stone, with which he advanced toward his sweetheart. "Just you tell me you've got lockjaw," he said, "and I'll crush your skull!"

26

THE MAID had been using, surreptitiously, the bathtub of her employer, an elderly bishop. He was a bachelor, very fastidious about his toilet, and desired the exclusive use of his tub. He reprimanded the maid with much indignation. ❡ "What distresses me most, Mary," he said, "is that you have done this behind my back."

27

BECKY came to her father with her head downcast. "Papa," she said, "you know that rich Mr. Leventhal? Well, he knocked me up, and I'm going to have a baby soon." ❡ "My God," said the father, "where is he, I'll kill him, the bastard, the moiderer, the son-of-a-bitch. Give me his address. I'll moider him." Dashing to the rich man's home, he cornered him, and, in a loud voice, told him what he intended to do. But the rich Mr. Leventhal was quite calm. ❡ "Don't get excited," he said, "I ain't running away, and I intend to do the right thing by your daughter. If she has a child and it's a boy, I'll settle on her fifty thousand dollars. If it's a girl, I'll settle thirty-five thousand on her. Is that fair?" ❡ The father halted, while the look of anger on his face changed. "And if it's a miscarriage," he pleaded, "will you give her another chance?"

28

E DELSON had retired from business and was enjoying life, till one day his eldest son came to him and demanded ten thousand dollars. ❡ "I knocked up a girl," he said, "and I got to have it, or there'll be terrible trouble. You must save the family name." ❡ "This is terrible," said the old man, "but I can't see the family disgraced. "Here is my check." Several days later his other son came to him. "Papa," he said, in an agonized voice, "I got to have twenty thousand. I knocked up a girl and if I don't have the money we are all ruined." ❡ "*Gevald*," said the father, "that takes away nearly mine whole fortune. But I can't see the family name disgraced. Here's the money." ❡ A few days later his daughter came to him and confessed, "Papa, I'm pregnant." ❡ "Thank God, business is picking up," said the old man.

29

ONE OF the earliest jokes is the tale told on the Emperor Agrippa, who, observing a slave pass the palace, was surprised to see that he was almost the image of himself. "Ho, there," the Emperor cried, "Slave, did your mother ever pass this way?" ❡ "No, sire, but my father did," was the rejoinder. ❡ This ancient jest is repeated in various languages, with the answer sometimes: "My father was your father's butler."

30

MANY stories are told of passionate men who have had recourse to animals. One of these pertains to a fella who entered his employer's barn and screwed a she-mule. As he was working away, just before the ejaculation, he was heard to exclaim, "Oh, if you only could cook!"

31

"I'M SURE my husband isn't faithful to me," an Irish-woman remarked. "Not one of the children look like him."

32

A TRAVELLING man who "made" a small town in the West, in the gold rush days, had been without his piece for some time. He inquired of the hotel clerk where he could obtain a woman. ❡ "There ain't none," said the clerk. "We use that mule in Perkins's barn." ❡ "What do you mean, you screw a mule?" asked the drummer. ❡ "Certainly," said the hotel man, "there's a fellow at the door, you pay him a dollar and screw the mule." So the travelling salesman went to the barn, and saw the black man at the door. Peeking in, he saw the mule, all decked out in ribbons, smelling of the best of perfumes. He took out a dollar and proffered it to the guardian. "There ain't nothin' doin'," said the guard, refusing the money. "Jim McCann, the gambler, is keepin' her now."

33

PAT AND MIKE were tired of war, and in a lull in the firing spied a cow, which they killed and skinned. Pat got into the hindquarters and Mike into the fore. Thus they proceeded back of the lines. Suddenly Mike in the forepart, began to run, Pat, perforce, following. They ran on and on, until Mike suddenly stopped. "It's no use, Pat," he gasped. "Brace yourself, here comes the bull."

34

A CERTAIN tragedian, noted for the size of his jock, was invited by a flapper to her home. As they sat in the parlor she begged for one look at the actor's immense tool. He unbuttoned his trousers and the maiden took the huge implement in her hand and commenced fondling it. ❡ "My, how lovely!" she said. "It's no wonder everyone calls him Caesar. How

regal he is in his dimensions. How imposing is his sta-
ture. How determined of purpose he is. Such fine line!
Such force of character. . ." ❡ The tragedian interrupted her: "I come to bury Caesar, not to praise him."

35

THE LAZIEST fellow in forty-eight States is rightly said
to be the one who was discovered by his employer
seated on a barrel, screwing a mule, but without moving
himself. All he was saying was, "Giddap, whoa, back! Giddap, whoa, back!"

36

A COCKNEY, strolling across Westminster bridge met
a whore, with whom he rapidly struck a bargain.
It being a dark night, she leaned against the bridge
parapet and lifted her skirts, while the cockney tried to
get his cock in. He worked away madly for a few
seconds seeking the opening. In the distance the lights
of London loomed soft and mellow. A clock chimed
the hour. Soft breezes blew over the Thames. All the
city was at peace,—the cockney trying to find the happy
orifice. At last he gasped, "Is it in?" ❡ "No," said
the girl, "a little more to the Abbey, if you please."

37

BERNSTEIN returned home, and in high dudgeon began to upbraid his wife. "Who was here today?
Tell me!" he demanded. "Who is your lover? Tell me,

who came here today to see you?" His wife's denials
availed her nothing. ⟨ "Don't try to fool me," Bernstein stormed, "I'm the only man in this house. Who
was your lover here today? Why is the toilet seat up!"

38

A COUPLE of bookmakers, standing in front of the
Hotel Astor turned to look after a "Follies" girl
who passed. "Gee," said one, "I feel like screwing that
dame again." ⟨ "What!" said the other, "you mean
to tell me you screwed that swell dame?" ⟨ "No,"
was the answer, "but once before I felt like it."

39

O LE AND PAT had struck up an acquaintance on ship-
board, working their way to this country, and, although their occupations did not permit them to see
much of each other it developed into a sort of friend-
ship. Pat was one of the deck crew, and it was Ole's
job to wet down the coke used in the engine room,
to keep the dust from choking the firemen. ⟨ Some
time after the ship docked the two friends met on
Broadway. After a few minutes of hearty greeting
Pat asked Ole: "Say, what the hell was it you were
doin' to work your way over, Ole?" ⟨ "Ay bane coke
soaker," said the Swede. ⟨ "Ye dirrty divil," said Pat,
spitting, "and I nivit suspicted ye!"

40

T WO CATS, screwing on the roof of a whore house,
fell off in their frenzy. A small boy rushed into

the sporting house and shouted to the madam: "Missus, your sign fell off."

41

H E: I wonder why that girl giggled when we passed her? ❡ She: Oh, don't you know? She works in the laundry."

—'Small town stuff.'

42

A LDERMAN Brown was reputed to have the longest prick in his town, and every married, and nearly every unmarried, woman in his ward was aware of it. A new resident was apprised of the Alderman's endowment and determined to test it. On approaching him, however, she found the Alderman not readily inclined to fall in with her ideas. ❡ "I'm all through with that stuff," he declared. "It's coming near to election and I can't take any chances." But the lady pleaded and pleaded until he yielded, and the quicker to satisfy her, took her into the hallway of her home. ❡ 'Now let's see how big your john really is,' the woman thought. "Unbutton my pants," said the Alderman, "we'll let this be all your work. Now take it out. Lift up your skirt. Put the head into your slot. All ready? Now— walk towards me!" Truly a prodigious weapon.

43

T O OBSERVE for herself, at first hand, the life of a chorus girl, a certain society matron ventured backstage during the performance of a musical play. As she stood near one of the chorines she nodded towards a man in shirt sleeves, with a black cigar in his mouth, and whispered: "Who is that?" ❡ The chorus girl extended her arm. "That dirty son-of-a-bitch, that lousy cock-sucking bastard, that whoremaster fairy," she said, "excuse me for pointing . . . is the stage manager."

44

TWO GIRLS met on Broadway and exchanged greetings. "What are you doing now?" asked one. Oh, I've got a swell job," was the answer. "I get in at noon, do very little work, the boss takes me for lunch, and then for a drive in the afternoon. In the evening, mostly, we take dinner at a road house. What are you doing?" ❡ "Oh, I'm a whore too," the other answered.

45

THERE was a fire in a whore house and one of the firemen managed to bring out a bed. ❡ "Thank God, they saved the workbench," said the madam.

46

JONES brought home a parrot which he said he had bought at auction, and which was supposed to be a wonderful bird. But for over two months neither Jones nor his wife, who had at first objected to Poll, could make the pet talk. They tried everything from "Polly wants a cracker," to "Hello, Polly, pretty Polly" but with no result. They concluded the bird was deaf and dumb. ⓪ One afternoon, while the head of the house was in his office Mrs. Jones invited the ladies of the. sewing circle to her home. One of them interrupted the gossip to state that she had secured a fine pair of hose at Bimble's, and lifted her skirt to show them. Another showed a marvelous corset she had purchased at West's. A third showed a neat silk petticoat. Mrs. Jones lifted her skirt and said: "Look at these wonderful bloomers, all silk, that I bought at Daltman's." The parrot, who had cocked his head from one to the other of the ladies now chirped up: "Ah, home at last. One of you whores give me a cigarette."

47

I N ORDER to start a small bank account for his wife, Brown agreed to give her fifty cents every time he diddled her. Mrs. Brown always dropped the money into a small safe she kept in her closet. At the end of the year the box was opened, to see how much money the lady would be able to put into the bank. Brown was amazed to see a number of one, five, and ten dollar bills among his halves. "Here," he said, "I only gave you a fifty cent piece each time I screwed you. How did you get these big bills?" "Do you think everybody is as stingy as you?" Mrs. Brown answered.

48

T HEY were in bed and he begged her to spread her thighs wider apart. She obliged, but still he begged her: "Spread them a little wider. Oh, just a little wider." Exasperated, she said to him: "What the hell are you trying to do, get your balls in?" ❡ "No," he answered, "I'm trying to get them out."

49

THE story is told of a clerk who married and spent a pleasant honeymoon with his bride. But one day he came to the office with a rather glum expression on his face. When his fellow clerks asked him what was the trouble he said: "Gee, I pulled a terrible bone this morning. Just before starting for the office I turned the wife off, and then, like an absent-minded jackass I laid down a five-dollar bill on the table." The other men consoled him. His wife wouldn't think anything of it, they assured him. ❡ "That isn't what bothers me," he answered. "She gave me three dollars change!"

50

THOMAS BURKE, author of *Limehouse Nights*, is the author also of the following, in his *Song Book of Quong Lee of Limehouse.*

OF POLITICIANS

Upon a time the amiable Bill Hawkins
Married a fair wife, demure and of chaste repute,
Keeping closely from her, however,
Any knowledge of the manner of man he had been.
Upon the nuptial night,
Awaking and finding himself couched with a woman,
As had happened on divers occasions,
He arose, and dressed, and departed,

Leaving at the couch's side four goodly coins.
But in the street,
Remembering the occasion and his present estate of
    marriage,
He returned with a haste of no dignity,
Filled with emotions of an entirely disturbing nature,
Fear that his wife should discover his absence
And place evil construction upon it,
Being uppermost.
Entering stealthily, then, with the toes of the leopard,
With intention of quickly disrobing, and rejoining the
    forsaken bride,
He perceived her sitting erect on the couch,
Biting shrewdly, with a distressing air of experience,
At one of the coins.

Even so it is when Big Politician meets Little Politician.

51

MINISTER: And how is my little lad today? ❡ Little Lad: Ssh! Not so loud. Dad might hear!

52

BERNSTEIN met Cohen on the street and seemed to be very angry. "Cohen," he yelled, "you got to make that boy of yours behave, or I'll break every bone in his body." Cohen demanded to know what had happened to cause this outburst. "He came to my house last night," said Bernstein, "and went with my daughter in the parlor. Like a good feller I left them alone. Now listen Cohen, I don't throw it up to you that he laid my Becky over on the couch. I don't throw it up to you that he screwed my Becky there; but what gets me real angry is why does the son-of-a-bitch have to wipe his cock on my plush portieres?"

53

THE HEAD salesman of the small town department store came forward to greet the customer. The latter demanded to see a pair of ladies' drawers with no pee-hole in them. The salesman showed him a pair. "How many of these have you?" the patron asked. "Two hundred pair," said the other. "Are there any more in town?" the stranger asked. When he was assured there were not, "I'll take all these," he said, and they were packed up for him. He paid, took the bundle to the street in front of the department store, saturated it with gasoline and set fire to the whole two hundred pair. ❡ The salesman rushed out in great trepidation. "Why did you buy all those buttonless drawers if you meant to burn them up," he cried. ❡ "Listen, I'm not crazy," said the customer, "I just don't want anybody else in this town to have the trouble I had last night."

54

A PHYSICIAN was very much annoyed by the frequent visits of a certain simple-minded fella who was always afraid something was the matter with him. One time he wanted a Wassermann, the next he thought he had piles. So it went week after week. One Monday morning, seeing Ronald present himself rather bloated with gas on the stomach, the idea suddenly came to the physician how he might get rid of this bothersome patient, and, at the same time, amuse himself. When the man unburdened himself of his symptoms he said gravely: "Ronald, you're caught at last. That has happened which I've long expected. From all you tell me and all I see you're certainly pregnant." "O M'God," the credulous fellow cried, and ran out in terror. As he passed the office of the only other doctor in the town, he ran in for a second consultation. The first physician had in the meantime telephoned his *confrère*, explained the situation, and been assured his joke would be upheld. "No doubt about it, Ronald, you're pregnant." By the time the fella reached home he was moodily resigned to his fate. He found his wife in the kitchen. "Becky," he petulantly reproached her, "I was afraid of what you'd do to me gettin' on top o' me like that."

55

A YOUNG woman came into Bimble's Department Store the other day and asked for a pair of drawers. "How do you want them to button?" the clerk asked, "front or side?" "Don't make no difference," the woman replied, "these here are for a corpse."

56

S EVERAL scientists were discussing prostitution, the customs esoteric and indigenous to its pursuit. Said one: "It must be exceedingly dissatisfying to a person of intelligence to observe the simulation of passion which a hardened prostitute offers to her patron. I have

often wondered whether there might not be some auto-
erotic means of inducing a real passion with each customer." ❡ The college janitor, who was standing
nearby interrupted: "You means you wants to know
how to get a whore hot?" "Yes," said the professor.
❡ "To get a whore hot, real hot," said the janitor,
"Fuck her and don't pay her!"

57

Life's Irony: One night with Venus. Six months
with Mercury.

58

How much do you charge?" the man asked.
❡ "Two dollars," said the whore. The bargain was made and they proceeded to her flat. ❡ She
lay over on the bed in the age-old posture of the prostitute, and he fitted to his erect prick a condom. When
he had finished he proferred her fee to her, but she
disdained it. "That ain't enough," she said. "But you
told me it was two dollars," said the man. "I know,"
the harlot answered, "but there's a dollar more—cover
charge."

59

In France a condom is known as *capote Anglaise*,
or "English cap." A gentleman once went into a
French shop, intending to purchase a dark cap, to
wear in mourning for his wife, who had recently died.
He knew the French word for cap was *capote*, so he

asked for that. Several were shown him, but he wanted
one English style, so he asked for a *capote Anglaise.*
The clerk sent him to the drug department where he
repeated his request to the lady clerk. She arched her
brows and asked him what color he wanted. "My wife
has just died," he answered, "so I want a black one."
❡ "Such delicacy!" said the clerk.

60

WHEN did Evelyn Nesbit Thaw really love her
husband? ❡ When he shot White.

61

A LITTLE girl came into a down-town drug store and
asked the clerk for three rolls of toilet paper.
The clerk, however, did not recognize the little one
and stopped her. "Who is it for?" he asked. ❡ The
little girl tilted her nose in the air as she answered:
"For all of us."

62

A T A STAG party on upper Broadway a sexpot was
giving a "circus." She lay stripped on a matting and
went through all the eye-rolling, bosom-heaving contortions
of a woman with a lusty man screwing her. She wriggled
her buttocks, locked and unlocked her thighs, squirmed and
tremored. Overcome with emotion one of the stags shouted:
"Fuck her hot!" The sexpot stopped and turned towards the
offender: "If you-all can't be gentlemen," she said, with
grave dignity, "this performance can't go on!"

63

Two reporters, seated in the Claridge dining room, amused themselves by guessing the occupations of the various diners. They decided to their mutual satisfaction that one was a broker, another an actor, a third a manager, a fourth a lawyer, and so on. But they disagreed about an elderly gentleman seated near a window, with a beautiful blond. One reporter insisted the old man must be a broker, while the other maintained he must be a physician. To settle the argument, one of the men called the old gentleman away from the girl, to their table. ❡ "To settle a bet," one of the newspapermen said, "would you mind telling us what your occupation is? My friend here says you are a broker, while my guess is that you are a doctor." The old gentleman surveyed them both a moment and replied, "I'm neither. I'm a taxidermist. Just now I'm stuffing that bird, and a little later I'll mount her."

64

At a Greenwich Village Ball a young woman presented herself entirely without clothes. The doorman stopped her, with these words: "Miss, this is supposed to be a costume ball. Now we don't mind how few clothes you have on, but you are supposed to represent something." The young woman retired to the ladies' dressing room, and shortly after reappeared with nothing on save a pair of black shoes and black gloves. The doorman again stopped her. "You're just as bad as you were before," he said, "what are you supposed to be?" ❡ "Can't you see?" the girl asked, "I'm the five of spades."

65

MAMIE: I'd like a little vacation, Missus. I want to go home and.see my children. Mistress: Why, Mamie, I didn't know you were married. Mamie: Well, I'm not, Missus. But I ain't been neglected.

66

THREE old maids went off on a tramp in the woods. The tramp died.

67

ONE 'Flapper' had just finished 'retailing'the latest. "Tell me another, Mame. I heard that one yesterday. It's a good one, though. I told it to Harry in bed last night and he laughed so hard he laughed his hard off.

68

MILLY JACKSON had long been noted in Tuscaloose as a peaceable, dutiful, and loving wife till one morning early one April she stood before the judge on a charge of having beaten her husband into insensibility. On hearing the charge against her, the minister of justice expressed his surprise. As the good woman was still panting with rage she had, however, no difficulty in eliciting her story, and less difficulty in pronouncing judgment. "You see, it was like this, Judge Brown. Yesterday I was doing my washing on the back porch like a good wife when my husband comes in from the field. And he sez to me, 'Milly, I want you to come into the house with me.' Being a dutiful wife, as yer honour knows, I went into the house with him. When we got into the house, he sez he wants me to come upstairs with him. So

I goes up stairs with him. 'Come on in here, Milly,' sez he. And I went into the bedroom with him. When I gets into the bedroom he sez, 'Milly, I want you to lay off all your clothes now.' So I lays off my clothes. 'Lay down on that bed,' then sez he. And I lays down. Now Judge, you knows me as a lovin' wife. But when that man gets me in that position and then says 'April fool' to me and walks out of the room, I figger that's more'n my lovin' can stand. I just had to do something." "Case dismissed," said the Judge dryly.

69

D o you know who earns most at this hospital, the rabbi or the priest?" queried the pretty nurse of the mother who had just been delivered of a boy. ❡ "No, I haven't the least idea." ❡ "You haven't? Why, the rabbi, of course. He gets all the tips." *

70

I n a gold-mining district, a claim-worker, a certain Brown, received news with which he was so delighted he ran down the street telling everybody he met that he had found a twelve-pound gold nugget as good as any to be found in America. Such news was without a precedent even in that locality where men were striking it rich every day. So the local newspaper sent a reporter to get the particulars. Mrs. Brown's

---

* Perhaps one of the last places one would expect to find the sexual joke is at the maternity hospital. Yet, due to the character of events there, as well as to a peculiarly compensative process at work in the nurses and in the women confined, the maternity hospital is for the sexual joke an especially favorable breeding-place. We only regret that we have no more examples of such 'cultures.'

elder sister, a lively hussy, fond of her joke, happened to answer the bell. This is the conversation that followed. ❡ "Does Mr. Brown live here?" ❡ "Yes." ❡ "May I speak with him." ❡ "I'm sorry, but he's not in just now. Is there anything I can do?" ❡ "Well, I understand he found a twelve-pound nugget." ❡ "Why, . . ." then, in a flash, seeing the situation, she added, "Yes." ❡ "Can you show me the exact spot where he found it?" ❡ "I'm afraid Mr. Brown would never consent to that, as it is private." ❡ "Is the hole very far from here?" ❡ "No, it is quite handy." ❡ "Has Mr. Brown been working the claim very long?" ❡ "Only about ten months." ❡ "Was he the first to work it?" ❡ "Well, he's told me he believed he was." ❡ "Was the work difficult?" ❡ "It was at first but it was easier after a while." ❡ "Has he got to the bottom yet?" ❡ "Not yet, I believe, but very near." ❡ "Do you think there are any more nuggets?" ❡ "Doubtless, if the claim is properly worked." ❡ "Has he worked it since he found the nugget?" ❡ "No. But last night I heard Mrs. Brown tell him it was time to start again." ❡ "I suppose he works secretly." ❡ "Yes, mostly at night." ❡ "Did he have any help?" ❡ "Well, Mrs. Brown did her level best, I am sure." ❡ "Do you think he would consider parting with the claim?" ❡ "No. He finds too much pleasure working it himself." ❡ "Did he blast with nitro-glycerine or did it do it all by hand?" ❡ "I believe he did some of it by hand. He just kept on digging, though I believe he used vaseline." ❡ "Has he widened the hole any?" ❡ "Yes, a little." ❡ "Is he going to improve the mine?" ❡ "Well, he said he would whitewash it. ❡ "Does he always work alone at night." ❡ "No. Mrs. Brown holds the tool for him and they go fifty-fifty." ❡ "Would you mind showing me the nugget?" ❡ "Not at all." ❡ *And she brought the baby to the door.*

71

L EVY was courting Reba and he sat on a chair. Reba sat in his lap. Her warmth made his peter rise, and Reba, sitting on it, felt it, and it was pleasant. So she sat a long time. Levy was in agony. But finally the door bell rang, and as the girl went to answer it, Levy shifted his jock to the other side. When his sweetheart returned, however, she sat on the other side, and again feeling the protuberance remarked, "Ooh, Abie, another one?" ❡ "Yeh," he answered foolishly, "I got two of them." ❡ When they were married Reba discovered his perfidy. "Now do it with the other one," she said, after her defloration. Abie told her he had given it to Feinberg. "He didn't had one," he said, "so I helped him out." A few days later Levy returned home early, in time to see his Reba coming out of Feinberg's flat. "What were you doing in there?" he demanded. ❡ "Aaah, Abie, you gave away the best one," she said.

72

A N ARMENIAN was being examined by the draft board. The physician, looking over the hunk's penis for traces of veneral disease, pulled back the foreskin. Unable to decide he let it slip back, and pulled it forward again. Absentmindedly he was continuing this operation when the draftee interrupted. ❡ "Pardon me," he said, "if you're doing this for the government go right ahead. But if you're doing it for me, move just a little faster, please."

73

TWO SALESMEN were standing in front of the Astor when a very beautiful girl passed. "Gee," said one, "I'd give a hundred dollars to smack that dame on the bare arse." ❡ "Do you mean it?" asked the other. "I know her, and maybe I could fix it for you." The first repeated his offer and his friend hurried after the girl. It was arranged, and the trio repaired to a room in the hotel. Here the young woman lifted her skirt, let down her bloomers and lay face down on the bed. The salesman who had made the offer gazed on her bare posterior with admiration. He allowed his hands to softly caress the rounded, warm flesh. ❡ "Gee," he said, "her arse is smooth like alabaster! Feel how round and warm it is. Man, it's wonderful!" ❡ "Go ahead, slap it," his friend exclaimed. ❡ "Why should I?" was the answer. "This feels wonderful, and it doesn't cost anything."

74

THE PRESIDENT of a large life insurance company was speaking at a company dinner. He had been speaking over two hours, and it was near midnight. Yet none of his employees had dared leave the room. There was a long list of speakers to follow, and these impatiently waited for the president to stop speaking. But he just rambled on, saying nothing at great length.

Finally, however, he sat down, after introducing the next speaker, a visiting English insurance man. The latter rose and said: "The hour has grown so late, gentlemen, that I will not deliver my speech, but will instead tell you a little story: A wee bird was flying about one day, when it suddenly began to rain. The downpour drenched the bird and it fell to earth, where the rain beat on it ceaselessly. Finally, towards noon the sun came out and warmed the little bird, so that it beat its wings and fluttered about. A horse passed by and dropped some breakfast for the wee bird, and it ate, and it ate till it could eat no more. Then straight into the air flew the wee bird, and, in good spirits, began to chirp. And it chirped and it chirped till a hawk, flying high in the sky, heard it, and swooping down on the little bird, gobbled it up. ❡ "And the moral of this little story," concluded the Englishman, to the president's discomfiture, "is, that when you're full of horseshit, don't chirp too much!"

75

THE DOCTOR had just delivered a young woman on the west side of a lovely child, and he complimented her, asking to see the father of such a wonderful baby. "I'm ashamed to admit it, doctor," said the young woman, "but my husband is on the road. The father of this child is Meyer Ginsburg." ❡ "Oho," thought the doctor, "one of those cases," and went on his way. In a few days he was called to confine a woman on the east side, and she also said the father of her child was Meyer Ginsburg. The following week a woman in Brooklyn attributed the parenthood of the child to

Meyer Ginsburg. In short the doctor answered about a dozen cases, in each of which the father was named Meyer Ginsburg. The last straw came when he was called to the Bronx to a family named Ginsburg, and delivered the woman of triplets. ❡ "Pardon me," said the doctor, "but is your husband named Meyer?" ❡ "Yes," answered the woman, "do you want to see him?. He's downstairs in the yard, sawing some wood." The doctor went down, to see this marvel, and found him a weazened little fellow. "Listen, Meyer," said the doctor, "I confined in the last few weeks twelve women in all parts of the city, uptown, downtown, east side, west side, Brooklyn, Queens and the Bronx, and each one said you are the father of the child. My God, man, how do you do it?" "It's easy, doctor," Ginsberg replied, "I got a bicycle!"

76

I T USED to be the custom of an ex-prize fighter to stand on the corner of Broadway and 45th Street and address young women who went by with this question: "Do you fuck?" A friend of his remonstrated with him. "Don't you get many a slap in the face?" he asked. ❡ "Yes," the pug answered, "but you'd be surprised what a lot of fucking I get, too."

77

M URPHY sought out the doctor, greatly worried. "My wife has a great pain inside at the end of the spine," he said. "I wish you'd give her something for it." The doctor gave him a powder, told him to

put it on the end of his penis, mount his wife, pene-
trate her, and thus rub the powder well into her. The
Irishman tried it, but returned to say that his wife
did not feel much better. "You didn't know how to do
it," the doctor told him. ❡ "Well, then, come on home
with me, and you do it," said the lout. The doctor did,
and finding the wife comely, was nothing loth to begin
and to rub the powder well in. Murphy looked on, and
scratching his head remarked, "If I didn't know you to
be the doctor, begorra, I'd think ye were screwing me
wife!"

78

I T WAS a cold night and the pimp was spending it with
his girl. They lay in bed, in her room, and disported
themselves right valourously, when there was a sudden
ring at the bell, repeated three times. They started.
It was a signal from a customer. "Where can I hide?"
asked the pander, looking about. "There isn't any
place in this room," said his girl, "but you better get
out of the way quick." There was no time for him to
do anything but grab a flimsy nightgown and rush out
on the fire-escape, before the patron arrived. ❡ The
bitter cold attacked the pimp out on the fire-escape, and
he trembled as he cursed himself for not getting a
heavier robe. His thin lips turned blue, his knees
knocked against each other till they hurt, his eyes grew
livid. Inside, where it was warm, the other man enjoyed himself at his leisure. It was cold outside, he
knew, so he was in no hurry to finish. ❡ Her lover,
meanwhile, began gradually to grow numb. He permitted himself a peek into the room, where, under the

warm sheets his lady and the cash customer were bob-
bing up and down. His nose had turned from red to
blue, he felt that his ears were non-existent, his fingers
were stiff rods, when finally he heard the door slam.
With difficulty he raised the window and intruding his
icy head into the warm room, asked, in a trembling
voice: "Has the *sucker* gone yet?"

79

A NDERSON's house was being over-run with rats and
he sought advice as to the best way to rid the
house of them. One friend advised that he bait a few
traps with apples to catch the rodents. On his way home
to try this method he met another friend, who advised
him to use nuts instead of apples, as bait. Perplexed,
he told his wife of the conflicting advice he had received. "Put down a few traps," she ansered, "with apples in some and nuts in the others. Then you're sure
to get them." ❡ He did so, and next day came up from
the cellar in great glee to break the news to his wife.
She was in the parlor, with a roomful of other women,
sewing, when he burst in. "I caught eight of them,"
he announced. His wife beamed on him. "Did you get
them by the apples?" she asked. ❡ "No."

80

A N ENGLISHMAN was present at a party once during which one of the guests recited a parody as
follows:
     "Mary had a little skirt,
       'Twas split just right in half,
       And everywhere that Mary went,
       She showed her little calf."

It was a jolly rhyme, thought the limey, and made a
mental note of it. Back in deah ol' Lunnon he essayed
to repeat it at a mixed gathering, promising it would
amuse the ladies. This is the rhyme as he read it:
  "Mary had a little, er, ah, skirt,
    'Twas slit, er . . dontcherknow, just in front,
    And everywhere that, er . . Mary went,
    She showed her little . .
My Gawd, *that* can't be right."

81

LULU was large, well-endowed, and took in washing.
One of her numerous beaux one day asked her: "How
come you got such big hands, Lulu?" "Why man," Lulu
replied, "when I was a child I used to make mud pies, and
the mud squashed out my hands like that." "Well, them,
how come you got such big feet?" her swain enquired.
"Why that was from walkin' barefoot in the mud," Lulu
answered. Her sweetie smiled, and asked: "Darlin', did you
ever *sit* in the mud?"

82

TWO FOREIGN traders, cast ashore on an island in the
South Seas, became aware that the native King was to
have a great birthday party. Each determined to bring him a
gift, to ingratiate himself with the royal host, and perhaps,
begin trade relations. Abie presented himself at the feast
with a huge bunch of bananas for the King. His Royal
Highness took one look, and laughed: "That's a hell of a gift
for ME! Take him outside and shove every one of those up
his arse." Abie was led off, but instead of fear, he was laugh-

ing. Asked to explain his uncalled for mirth, he replied:
"Mine brother is bringing pineapples!"

83

THEY met on the train, and to while away the time
a poker game was suggested. Repairing to a drawing room mutual introductions began. "My name is
Hancock," said one. An elderly gentleman introduced
himself as "Alcock." A third was named "Babcock."
"My name is Hitchcock," said a fourth. The fifth, a
weazened little fellow, said, "I don't think I care to play this
game. My name is Kuntz."

84

MAMIE was parading down the main street of the
poorer section of Birmingham, dressed fit to kill. She
had on resplendent ear rings, a new gown and wrap, her
shoes were patent leather, her hose silk. On her head was a
hat trimmed with birds of paradise. A friend accosted her:
"Why, Mamie, where did you get them beautiful togs?"
Mamie giggled back, "Ain't you heard? I've just been
ruined!"

85

THE REGIMENT was billeted in a neutral village just
over the border from the enemy. Two peasant
girls met in the market-place, and one said to the other:
"You know how we're trying to be nice to the soldiers.

Well, this morning the strangest thing happened. A private came into our house, where I was alone, and without a word took off his sword. Then he removed his coat, let down his trousers, and, still without a word, threw me on the bed and screwed me. Still silent he got up, redressed, bucked on his sword, and went out. . . Lord only knows what he wanted."—*From the Hungarian.*

86

THE AMERICAN version of the above story is that a chambermaid at the Biltvania answered a ring from the 16th floor. The moment she entered the room the guest seized her, threw her on the bed and did his will. Then, as expeditiously, he ushered her to the door and pushed her out. ❡ "To this day," the maid told a friend, "I don't know what he was ringing for."

87

A HOTEL chambermaid on her honeymoon wrote to her friend: "You ought to try it without your shoes, Mame, it's great!"

88

GOLDSTEIN's wife had died. Goldstein made the house ring with his lamentations. Finally his brother persuaded him to go to his room, to quiet himself. For three days nothing was heard from Goldstein. His brother, alarmed, went up to see him, and found him screwing the maid. ❡ "Meyer," he said, in an injured tone, "Only a few days your wife is dead, Meyer, and what are you doing?" ❡ Meyer stopped long enough to look up. He pleaded, "In my grief, I should know what I'm doing?"

89

Ronald was pained. With no malice aforethought he had returned home several hours earlier than usual, only to find his wife in bed with the janitor. "Minnie, Minnie," he said, "I sure am ashamed of you." But Minnie only looked up and said, "Look on, buster, gaze on and learn somethin'."

90

There is a parallel to this story telling how Levy came home early one day, to find his wife in bed under the vigorous strokes of a stranger. "Rebbeca!" said Levy, "to think that after all these years, after all I did for you, after I made from you a lady and gave you from the finest, you should do such a thing to me. Rebecca, I took you when you was a poor girl and . . . ain't you even got respect enough to stop while I'm talking to you?"

91

A gentleman from Idaho was in Paris and didn't want to make himself too conspicuous. So he asked a cabby to give him the address of a good whorehouse. He went there by himself, quietly, asked for a private room, and, after selecting his partner, ordered dinner with lots of wine.. After the meal the man entertained himself in various ways with his playmate, who taught him positions of which even Elephantis,

Aretino and Luisa Sigea were ignorant. Thoroughly drained, the gentleman from Idaho went downstairs, where he asked the madam what his bill was. ❡ "There is no charge," said the lady of the house. ❡ Astonished, but not disposed to argue the matter, her guest left. All next day he hugged his secret to himself. He could barely wait till dinner time before he again presented himself before the bawds. Again he went through his performance, but this time, when he made a bluff at paying the piper he was informed the charges were seven hundred francs. ❡ "What!" he shrieked. "Wasn't I here last evening, and didn't I go through every kind of screw, and you didn't charge me a sou?" ❡ "Ah," said the madam, "but last night was for the movies."

92

A BRAMS frantically dashed up the stairs of his home. "Sarah," he panted, "we got to move out of here right away. I just found out the most terrible thing. I just learned that the janitor from this house screwed every woman in it but one." ❡ "Yeh, know," said Sarah, "that's that stuck up thing on the third floor."

93

L ORD Cholmondely called his valet to him. "I'm bored this evening," he said, "Bring me a whore." ❡ His valet went on the errand and soon returned with a fairly presentable young English girl, blond-haired and blue-eyed. ❡ "Undress," said m'Lord. "Lie on that couch there." ❡ As the girl complied, he removed his waistcoat and trousers, and mounted her. He was

laboring with great diligence when the lady, to let him
have the thrill that went with each of her affairs, gave
him a moist tongue kiss. ❡ "Here now," said the
Lord, "don't get personal, or I shall jolly well stop
screwing you!"

94

TWO FELLOWS and their wives were on a train trip
when they passed through a tunnel. As they got into
the light Cohen said to Levy: "I just kissed your wife."
"That's nothing," said Levy as he put his fingers under
Cohen's nose. "Smell."

95

THE young man on his honeymoon had selected
what he thought to be a quiet hotel. What he
saw, however, in a room across the air-shaft from his
caused him to pull down the blind and call for the
manager. ❡ "What kind of a joint is this?" he demanded. "I come here with my bride, thinking this was
a quiet, refined hotel. What's the first thing I see
here?" He led the manager to the window and pulled
the blind aside. In the room across the way three nude
men were practicing a spinctrian posture, that is to say,
in vulgar language, back-scuttling each other. "Lucky
Julius," was his comment, "always in the middle."

96

SPEAKING of back-scuttling, the story is told of two
Armenians who were discussing the merits of various
positions for intercourse. ❡ "Did you every try the
back way?" asked one; and when the other said he

hadn't, he urged him, "When you get home tonight, try it on the wife. Gee, it's great, and you'll never go back to the other way." ❡ The second Armenian said he would try anything once. When they met the next day the first asked him how he liked the back way method. ❡ "Oh, it's very fine," the other answered, "but the children laughed so!"

97

WHILE on the subject it would be as well to tell the story of the two friends who worked in a laundry. One was always quite well dressed, the other shabby, although both earned the same wages. The prosperous one urged the other to do as she was doing. Listen," she said, "every night I go to a certain house on the next block, where I manage to earn a few dollars easy. Come on over, I'll introduce you." The other demurerd. A compromise was finally reached when her friend suggested that for a few days they go over during the lunch hour and try it. Her second day at her new vocation found the shabby laundress in the company of a hilarious youth who offered three times the usual fee if she would let him do it the back way. ❡ "Come on," he said, "just like a couple of dogs. It won't hurt you." ❡ "All right," the girl finally agreed, "but for heaven's sake don't drag me past the laundry."

98

AN OLD rounder married an innocent virgin, in the days when there were such creatures, and, tired of the various postures of love, determined, on discovering how demure his bride was, to begin by teaching her how to play the flute. For several weeks after his marriage he amused himself in this way. Then even that thrill waned, and one night as they ere abed he attempted to board his still virginal spouse. ❡ "You get off me!" she shrieked. "Don't you dare try to do that, you dirtly degenerate."

99

BUSINESS being slow, a travelling man accepted a position with a circus, and continued travelling. When the troupe was out about five weeks, and camped on a prairie, the salesman approached one of the ballyhoo men. ❡ "Say," he said, "what do you fellers do for a woman?" ❡ The ballyhoo man looked him over. "Why, hell," he said, "we never need a woman. We take any man on the lot. It's a shot for shot proposition." ❡ "What, buggery?" said the salesman. "Never!" ❡ But in a week he changed his mind and again approached his friend, to ask him just how to go about it. ❡ "Oh, go over to any man on the lot and tell him what you want," he was advised. ❡ Next day he sought the ballyhoo man and dragged him to one side. "Look at this," he said, taking out his tool, which was badly lacerated, and hung almost in shreds. "With a whole circusful to choose from, I had to pick the glass-eater!"

100

A COCKNEY had just been married. He hurried to a taxi with his bride, followed by a number of their friends. As they sank back into the seat one of his friends leaned in and leered at them. "What abaht

t'night?" he chuckled, "what abaht t'night?" "Yes,"
the bride shot back at him, "and what abaht this afternoon? Eh?"

101

WHEN I got back to the office my stenographer told
me she had a new position." ❧ "What did you
say?" ❧ "I said, 'Shut the door and let's try it.' "

102

A COUPLE who were fond of playing poker found it
inconvenient to cohabit because of their four-year
old son. So they formed the practice of waking each
other in the middle of the night to make approaches in
a code they agreed on, which made use of poker terms.
❧ At 1 A. M. she awoke and said, "I open." ❧ "I
pass," said he, turning over to sleep. ❧ At 3 A. M. he
awoke, and tapping his wife on the shoulder, said, "I
open." ❧ "I pass," said she. ❧ "But I've got a
straight," said he. ❧ She hesitated a moment. "All
right, I'll play," she said. "I need one to fill."

103

A NEW WORD was coined for a certain actor whose
inclinations were equally amorous for men as for
woman. One of his critics called him "ambisextrous."

104

HAVING come to an understanding with the farmer's
daughter, a certain travelling salesman sought to
find a convenient time and place for them to get to-

gether. As no opportunity offered itself, he determined to make one. The girl was not allowed to leave the house, so one morning while downtown the salesman procured a dog license. When he returned home they hid the old man's glasses and told him they had been married. "Here is the license, we're going upstairs to bed," said the drummer. ❦ The farmer, hunting around, found his glasses and hurried upstairs, where he pounded on the door. His daughter paused in her undressing. ❦ "Mamie," said the old man, "ef you hain't done it, don't do it, cause this ain't fer it! This ain't no doin' license!"

105

H EYWOOD BROUN in his book *The Boy Grew Older* has his hero, Peter Neale, take home a chorus girl who lives on 168th Street. At her door she says to him, "You're entitled to a kiss. Anyone that takes me all the way to 168th street is entitled to at least a kiss from me. Next month I'm going to move to 242nd Street!"

106

A MARRIAGE-BROKER was trying to arrange a match between a business man and a beautiful young girl. But the business man was obdurate. "Before I buy goods from a mill I look at snatches, and before I get married I must also have a sample," he said. ❦ "But, my God, you can't ask a virtuous, respectable girl for a thing like that," said the *schadchen*. ❦ "I'm a man from business," said the other, "and that's the way it will be done, or not at all." ❦ The broker went

off in despair to talk with the girl. "I got for you a
fine feller, with lots of money," he said. "He's a business man and his rating is O. K. But he's *eppis a little
meshuga*. He says he's a good business man, and
wouldn't go into nothing blind. He must have a sample." ℂ "Listen," said the girl. "I'm so smart a business man as he is. Semples I wouldn't give him. Ref-
erences I'll give him!"

107

Prix: Do you know why Jesus was born in a stable?
ℂ Bollix: No, why? ℂ Prix: Because they didn't
allow Jews in the hotels.

108

Two Swedish chambermaids went to a photographer.
He ordered them to stand facing the camera, with
their backs to a painted scene. Not satisfied with their
position, he kept shifting them until one of the girls
asked the other, "Why don't he take the picture? What
is he doing?" ℂ "He wants to focus," said the other.
ℂ "Let him take the pitcher first," her friend replied,
"and foke us after."

109

A learned sexologist was once asked by a patient
what was the ideal time for a screw between man
and woman, husband and wife. ℂ "A man should sleep
in a bed by himself in one wing of his house, the bed
being in the middle of the room, which should not have
a carpet. The wife should be in another wing, con-

nected by a long, uncarpeted hallway, with stone flag-
ging. Now, when the husband will get up, naked, from
his warm bed, walk quietly down that hallway, to a
door, which will be in the middle, separating the couple,
and wait without making a sound for his wife to get out
of her warm bed, and walk naked down the cold hall
to the door . . . that, that, I say, will be the highest
moment of desire, and the right time for a screwing
party!"

110

H e's so dumb he went into the Martha Washington
Hotel and asked for the gent's toilet.

111

H e's a spendthrift all right. He's keeping a woman
at the Y. W. C. A.

112

S oon after the Hall-Mills murder case the Methodist
Episcopal College of New Jersey met, according to
Will Rogers, and passed a ruling that hereafter all rec-
tors must button their collars in front, and their pants
behind!

113

W hen the Singer Midgets go on a vaudeville tour
the house work is divided among them. One of
the ladies cooks, another sews, one of the men does

the heavy work, and so on. One week, while they were playing the Palace theatre in New York, the lady who did the cooking missed a couple of performances. Newspapermen who approached Walter Kingsley, house press-agent, scenting a possible story, were told that the midget who did the family washing in a kettle had had the ill fortune to fall backward into it. ⁋ "Was she badly hurt," Kingsley was asked. ⁋ "No, she just got a little behind in her work," he said.

114

A NOTORIOUS 'piss customer' ambled into Dinty Moore's place but was promptly shooed out. He tried another cafe, but, being as well known there, he was again put out. After four or five attempts, his bladder full to bursting, he rushed into the office of a Times Square doctor. ⁋ "I can't piss, doctor, I can't piss," he moaned. ⁋ "Here, come with me," said the doctor, leading him to the toilet. "Now try hard." ⁋ The man nearly filled the bowl with his water. "What do you mean," said the physician, "you piss all right. Why did you say you couldn't?" ⁋ "I meant they wouldn't let me," said the man, gratefully.

115

O NE season when a famous actor returned to London from a tour of the provinces he decided to cut expenses, so dismissed his leading man and engaged a cheaper actor. He had occasion a few weeks later to use a comfort station and noticed, after defecating, that the attendant was the former leading man. "My, how you have fallen," he said as he

paid the man his fee. "You must be starving to do this."
"Oh, it isn't as bad as that," said the actor. "Of course,
business has been a little slow this morning. I've had twelve
pissers, and you're the third shit to come in."

116

"**B**UGS" BAER says: "God put the stink in a fart for
guys who are hard of hearing."

117

A WEEK before the wedding the young girl came to
her mother in tears. "I'm so afraid about getting
married," she said. "I'm afraid I won't be able to
please my sweetheart." ❡ Her mother, who wanted to
make the girl's trials easier, undertook to explain to
her the secrets of married life. With some hesitation,
she began to explan to the girl what she would have to
go through. ❡ "Oh, that doesn't bother me, mother,"
said the daughter, "I can fuck alright, but I can't cook."

118

A FELLOW who had the misfortune to get his first clap
went to his doctor. To frighten him the doctor said:
"I'm afraid I'll have to cut off your organ." "My which?"
asked the fellow. "Your organ," said the doctor. "So that's
what you call it," said the guy. "Can I have a minute to
myself to think this thing over?" The doctor agreed. In a
few moments he came back into the room, to hear the poor
man addressing his penis: "Organ o' mine, you have played
your last tune!"

119

THE schooner *Salt Lake* had been at sea over a month and was nearing Tahiti. The crew were as horny as could be, but one of the men, who had never visited the port was disturbed as to how he should get what he was after. He approached the mate. ❡ "It's simple," said the latter. "When you go ashore just go up to the first man you see and ask him where you can get a woman." ❡ "But I can't speak the bloody language." ❡ "Well, in that case just take out fifty cents and show him your prick. He'll direct you then all right." ❡ In a few hours the sailor returned. "That was lousy advice you gave me," he told the mate. "The first guy I went up to, I took out my pecker, and showed him half a buck. In a second the bastard had his prick out, with fifty cents, matched me, and took the buck!"

120

WHEN the animals boarded the ark, old Noah, to prevent trouble, made all the males check their organs, giving each a ticket for his private property. When they were settled on Mt. Ararat, just before going ashore, when their parts would be restored to them, the monkey approached his spouse. ❡ "Tonight, my dear," he said, "I'm going to give you a real nice time. I don't mind telling you it'll be the best you ever had. I've swiped the elephant's ticket."

121

A MICHIGANITE, who had just purchased one of Mr. Ford's latest, was out for a drive one day when the car suddenly halted and he could not get it started again. Just then Henry himself drove by in a Lincoln, saw the man's difficulty and stopped. ❡ "I can't seem to turn the engine over," the customer complained. Ford himself lifted the head, leaned down into the mechanism and whispered to it. Immediately the engine began to run. ❡ "Oh, Mr. Ford, please tell me what you told the engine," the man pleaded, "so I won't have this trouble again." ❡ "I just whispered 'Lizzie, this is Henry, turn over,'" said the great historian.

122

"I'M GOING to buy a Studebaker," an old maid said to a friend of hers. ❡ "Don't do it," he counseled, "Get a Buick. If you buy a Studebaker, you'll get screwed." ❡ Next day she had a Studebaker.

123

A PROFESSOR of botany was lecturing to a girl's class. "This twig, you will notice," said he, "is composed of bark, hardwood, and pith. Of course you know what pith is." ❡ The class stared at him blankly. "Don't you know what pith is?" the professor repeated. "You, Miss Brown, you know what pith is, do you not?" ❡ "Yeth, thir," said Miss Brown.

124

"NO, YOU'RE not going out tonight," said Mrs. Kantor, to her daughter. "I wouldn't let you should go." ❡ "But mamma, how do you expect I should get a feller if I don't go to parties and balls?" complained the girl. ❧ "Never mind," said the mother, "you'll get a feller without parties,—you'll get a feller without balls. . . ."

125

A SCHADCHEN, or marriage broker, was telling a prospect about a splendid girl he had in mind for him to marry. "She's got a college education. She's beautiful,—take a look from this picture. Money in the bank she's got too. Her family is A1, and her disposition is fine." ❧ "I know," said the young man, "but why do you give me such a bargain. What's the matter with her?" ❧ "Nothing," said the *schadchen*, "only, she's the least little bit pregnant."

126

A STRANGER was being shown through a small southern town. The bank, it was pointed out to him, was owned by Mr. Cowen. So was the department store, and the town garage. "That's a beautiful fountain," said the stranger. "Cowen put that up," his guide said, "and that library too." "Cowen must be well liked and respected in this town," said the stranger. "Only for one little mistake he made!" the cicerone said. "If not for that one little mistake people would now be pointing him out as 'Cowen, the philanthropist,' instead of 'Cowen, the cocksucker.' "

127

T HE young man and his sweetheart sat in the parlor. Her parents, who were in the kitchen, noticed that the youth kept running to the bathroom every few moments. "What's the matter with him?" the old man asked. "I don't like this running business. Maybe he's got a disease. Go on, Becky, you ask him what's the matter with him." ⁋ With some hesitation the mother approached him and asked him why he kept running to the bathroom so often. ⁋ "Well, I'll tell you," the young man replied. "You're daughter is so lovely that I can't help having an erection every time I see her. So I've been running into the bathroom to put cold water on the head of my thing, to keep it down." ⁋ The old woman returned to her husband. "*Nu*," he asked. "What kind a disease is he got?" "You should have such a diseases," she said.

128

Prix: Why is an old car like a whore? Bollix: I don't know. Why? Prix: Because you can have lots of fun with one, but you'd hate to be seen in public with it.

129

Frank Harris, the writer, disgusted with Oscar Wilde for his passion for young boys, finally made the author promise to abstain. However, not two weeks later he called on Wilde and found the latter in bed, with a boy. "You son-of-a-bitch," said Harris, who was never known to use the polite term when the impolite would do just as well. "What the hell do you mean by this? Didn't you promise me on your word of honor that you'd never do this again?

Didn't you tell me you were going to turn over a new leaf?"
"Don't get excited, Frank, I am," said Wilde, unabashed.
"Can't you see I'm at the bottom of the page now?"

130

"WHAT'RE you doing for a living now, honey?" a
sweet young thing asked of her beau. "I'm a lion
tamer," he answered modestly. "For two bucks a day, I
stick my head in the lion's mouth." "You ain't no lion
tamer," said his sweetie. "You're just a lyin' bastard."

131

COMING home from a party the young man and his
girl stopped in her hallway for a parting kiss. As
they embraced he grew horny, and pleaded with her to
lift her skirt. She refused. He tried every artifice to
excite her orifice, but with no success. Finally, in sheer
disgust he left her, saying, "You won't, eh? Well,
there's no use the three of us standing here then."

132

SI CAME to New York armed with an address which
a travelling man had given him and the admonition
to 'ask for Singer and say Jack sent you.' Everything
went well, and Si spent a delirious night. Next day he
was walking down lower Broadway, when to his surprise he saw the magic name Singer on a store window,
with some sewing machines on exhibition. Inside, behind a counter stood a pretty girl. ❡ "Jack sent me,"
beamed Si as he entered. ❡ The girl smiled at him

and said, "Would you like one?" ❡ "You bet. How much?" asked Si. ❡ "Well, some are eighty dollars, some sixty-five, and the cheapest are fifty." ❡ "Go on," objected Si, "what you trying to do. I got one last night for twenty dollars." ❡ "Oh," said the girl, "that's the kind you screw on a table." ❡ "No, ma'am," insisted Si, "I screwed this one in bed!"

133

Jock: I saw a funny thing on Broadway today. A rooster was chasing a chicken down the street in front of the Columbia theatre, trying to mount her. But the chicken ran from him, out to the middle of the street and stuck her head on a trolley track, and was run over. ❡ Stropp: What was the big idea? ❡ Jock: Better death than dishonor.

134

Two fellows who hadn't seen each other in some time met one day and one asked the other what he was doing. "Oh, me, I'm a lion tamer," he said. ❡ "What do you mean, a lion tamer?" chaffed the other. ❡ "Well, you see," said the friend, "I go into the lion's cage with a whip, and when I swing it to the right, the lion rolls over on his right side, and when I swing it to the left, he rolls over on his left side." ❡ "Suppose you whip it straight down in front?" asked the other. ❡ "Gosh, you don't do that, because then the lion leaps right at you!" ❡ "What do you do in a case like that?" ❡ "Why then, the only thing to do is to put your hand down inside your trousers, grab a lump of shit and fling it in his face." ❡ "Huh!

Where will you get the shit?" ❡ "Don't worry, it'll be there, it'll be there."

135

A STORY that, with many others, is attributed to Mark Twain gives the famous answer to a foolish question. ❡ "What do you think of Patti?" Twain was asked, according to this version of the yarn. Patti at the time was at the height of her success. ❡ "Well," Twain drawled, "I'd any time rather lie down next to Patti, naked, than next to General Grant, in full uniform."

136

A YOUNG veterinary in the South was called in a hurry to attend a horse, but by the time he arrived the animal was dead. He asked the farmer if he might not take certain parts of the horse with him, to preserve in alcohol, so he might have them in his office. The farmer allowed him to and the vet. cut out the heart, liver, prick and balls of the horse, and threw them into the back of his buggy. As he drove home over a rough road, the prick and balls were shaken out and lay in the road. A couple of local girls chanced to pass. They stopped to look, and one said in awe-stricken tones: "See what happened to some guy who was playing around too much!"

137

THE famous Manhattan Cheese Club was in session, and the various newspapermen who belonged to it were discussing the Indian custom of *suttee*. "When

an Indian dies his body is laid on a huge funeral prye,"
said one of the men, "and the widow throws herself
living into the flames." ❡ "I wonder why she does
that," another of the writers asked. ❡ "I guess the
reason is," a prominent humorous writer answered, "it's
the first time in years she's seen the old man real hot."

138

J ONES had been cast on a desert island, without even
one of the much discussed dozen books, and for
three months he had managed to exist on the ship's
stores he had saved and on wild fruits and roots. In
all that time he had not seen another human being.
Consider his surprise, then, one day to discover a beautiful woman walking towards him. ❡ "How long have
you been on the island," she asked him, after he had
approached and spoken to her. ❡ "Three months," he
answered. "It's funny we never met before. We need
not have been lonely, if we had met." ❡ "Well," said
the woman, "you meet me tonight and I'll give you
something you haven't had in three months." And she
smiled archly. ❡ Jones could scarcely restrain himself
till the appointed time. The lady met him, with her
finger to her lips in an attitude of caution. "Follow
me," she whispered, "and you'll get what I promised
you . . . something you haven't had in three months.
It's the finest Scotch you ever tasted!"

139

"B OY," said one fellow to another, "I just come from the
doctor. He jabs me full of mercury, he does. I feel
heavy like lead." "Boy, you ain't got nothin' in you," said

the other. "I've got what you might call mercury in me. I've got so much, in fact, that I'm nine foot two inches tall in the summertime."

140

JAMES BRYANT tried to enlist in the navy during the war, and applied for examination to recruiting headquarters, 280 Broadway. He was ordered to strip, and one of the naval doctors listened to his heart with a stethoscope, tapped him on the stomach, put his ear to his back, tested his vision and so forth. Then to see whether he had piles he said to him: "Bend over," which the fellow did. "Now pull the cheeks of your arse apart," ordered the navy doctor. ❧ "What, so soon, Admiral?" plaintively asked Bryant.

141

THE waitress leaned over the table and asked the diners what they would like for dessert. One ordered one dessert, another something else. ❧ "I'll take raisin pie," said Jones. ❧ "And you?" asked the waitress, leaning over the table to the last one. He caught one glimpse of her well-developed, white breasts, and said, "Mine's raisin' too."

142

ONE OF Ford's stockholders had a dream one night in which Henry presented himself at the gates of Heaven and St. Peter asked him why he sought admission. ❧ "Because I produced a machine," said Ford,

"which gave great pleasure to most human beings."
A loud fart from within the gates greeted this state-
ment. ⁅ Ford looked up in anger and asked who had
saluted him thus. ⁅ "Me," said a voice, "Adam. I'm
the guy that invented the machine that gives the greatest
pleasure to the saps down below. I invented woman."
⁅ "Well, maybe you're right," said the deceased De-
troiter, in this dream, "but you certainly know nothing
of mechanical principles. For one thing, you put the
exhaust too near the intake!"

143

"WHY IS a Ford car called a Henry in Detroit
and a Lizzie in New York?" ⁅ "Because by
the time it gets to New York it loses it's nuts."

144

THE following rhyme recently went the rounds of
the Algonquin Club:
> There are so many feather beds,
> So many little maidenheads,
> There's practically no excuse
> For sodomy, or self abuse.

145

AN OLD man overheard some young fellows talking
of the women they had but recently screwed.
"Gee," said one, "the dame I had last night hollored
to beat the band. I hurt her somethin' awful with my
screwing." ⁅ The others also declared that so fierce
had been their fervor that they too had hurt the last

few girlies they had fucked. The old man—we may as
well give you his name, you've probably guessed it by
now, Jake Shubert—murmured to himself: "Gosh, it's
years since any girl I screwed said I hurt her. I wonder if I still can?" So he called up one of the Winter
Garden girls, threw her on his couch and began to screw
her. ❡ "Ouch," she shrieked. Jake beamed. ❡ "Am
I hurting you?" he asked, with exultation. ❡ "Yes,"
screamed the girl, "you're stepping on my foot!"

146

THE summer boarders had begun to arrive at the
little farmhouse in the mountains. The first one
up noticed that the farmer's wife carried in her arms
an infant. "So," he said, "we none of us suspected you."
❡ "It isn't my child," said the woman, "it's my daughter Marie's." ❡ "What?" said the boarder, "little
Marie? She's such a child. When did she get married?"
❡ "Oh, my, no," said her mother, "she's not married.
She's much too young for that."

147

ZIEGFELD chorus girls were sent on a hunt recently for
a book called *Life of an Indian Princess* by Youcan B.
Tan!

148

THE favorite story of the late Tom Oliphant, first
president of the Manhattan Cheese Club, was
about the young man who took his sweetie to a hotel,
and, as they were both stripped, she suddenly began to

tremble. "I've got an attack of St. Vitus dance," said she, shivering all over. Her escort 'phoned down for a few bellboys, who hurried to the room. The young woman was in bed, shuddering wildly. ❡ "Grab her arms," yelled the young man to a couple of the bell hops. "You grab her legs. Hold tight now." As they held the girl thus he calmly climbed into bed, mounted the girl, put his prick way into her and yelled to the straining bellboys, "Let 'er go!"

149

EVERYBODY is familiar with the story of the boy who was seen masturbating himself in the barn. He was overheard to say, as he looked at the ejaculation in his hand, "You might have been a barber, a farmer, or a travelling man. You might have been a merchant, a thief, a wise man, or even President. But now, well . . . " as he suddenly gobbled it down, "I'll give you another chance."

150

AMONG the many dirty stories told about a certain beautiful actress, as they have been told about every beauty from Eve up, is the one about her manager. He discovered one day that his star had been selling her coynte (to use a certain elegantism), at a hundred dollars a screw. Now he had long desired her, but had never suspected that she might be obtainable. So he approached her. ❡ She agreed to spend the night with him, but on the same terms as her other lovers, one hundred dollars. Rudolph agreed and that night she came to his apartment, after her performance at the Casino. ⟨ He screwed her at midnight. At one o'clock she was awakened and again screwed. A half hour later the performance was repeated. The star marvelled at his virility. Her wonder increased when again, at the end of a little time she was vigorously screwed. ⟨ "My, Rudolph," she said, "but you're strong!" ⟨ "I'm not Rudolph," a strange voice answered, "he's at the door taking tickets!"

151

There was on old woman who lived in a shoe
She had so many children, she didn't know what to do.
                              —*Mother Goose.*
There was another old woman who lived in a shoe,
She didn't have any children—She knew what to do!
                              —*Mother Goose Revised.*

152

A MAN came into a drug store and asked for a condom. In an hour he returned and asked for half a dozen. Two hours later he came in and bought a dozen. "What's the idea?" asked the clerk, "are you ripping them?" ⟨ "No," the man answered. "I've decided to stay all night."

153

Two Irishmen passed a drug store in which was displayed an advertisement for *Hunyadi Janos*,— 'Makes you Young Again'. They decided to try it. Each had a glass of the stuff and sat down to await developments. After a few minutes Pat said: "Do ye feel any younger, Mike?" ⟨ "Divil a bit," responded the other in approved joke-book Irish. ⁋ So they had another drink, and after a few moments Pat again asked Mike if he felt younger. Again the other answered in the negative, and they had another drink of Hunyadi. ⁋ After a pause Mike turned to Pat and said with a wan smile, "Pat, it's worrked. I've just done a childish thing." ⁋ "Ye have? What?" asked his friend. ⁋ "I've just shit in me pants," said Mike.

154

"I'M GOING to a first night tonight, doctor," said a young woman patient; "and you know how the different dramatic critics have been railing against people who sneeze or cough in the theatre. Now I'm troubled with fits of sneezing and coughing, and I want you to give me something so that I won't annoy Heywood Broun or Alexander Woolcott." ⁋ "Drink this," said the doctor, offering her a glass. The young woman did, and then, mouth awry, asked the physician just what it was. ⁋ "That's a double dose of Pluto water," he answered. "Now you won't dare sneeze or cough."

155

A LASCIVIOUS young priest used to hear confession in his own rooms,—when the girl was beautiful. There came to him one time a sweet but shy morsel, who hesitated to unburden her soul. "Did the young man do this?" he asked, putting his arms about her. ⁋ "Yes, father, and worse," the girl replied. ⁋ "Did he do this?" asked the priest, kissing her. ⁋ "Yes, father, and worse." ⁋ "Did he do this?" lifting her

skirt and touching her up. ❦ "Yes, father and worse."
❦ By this time, the priest, maddened, threw the girl
onto a couch and inserted his penis. "Did he do this?"
he managed to ask. ❦ "Yes, father, and worse," came
the answer. ❦ When the man of God had finished
fucking the girl he asked, "You say he did this too,
and *worse?* Now what worse could he have done?"
❦ "I think, father," said the shy, young girl, "that
he gave me a clap."

156

A CHAP was rowing down the Thames one Sunday
when he lost one of his oars and drifted out to
midstream. He tried to paddle with the other but
found it difficult. Just then, coming downstream he
noticed a boat with a man and two women in it, all rowing. ❦ "I say," he shouted across the water, "lend
me one of your oars." ❦ "The other man looked up
indignantly.   "They're not 'ores," he protested.
"They're me mother and sister."

157

A GRAY-HAIRED old gentleman came into a whorehouse and asked the Madam for Mary. The girl
happened to be out, so the lady of the house asked
him if Molly, or Jane, or Edna wouldn't do as well.
"They're all blonde, and about her height," she said.
But the old man shook his head. No, they wouldn't
do. ❦ The Madam tried to interest him in some of
the other inhabitants, without success. Finally, in ex-
asperation she turned from him. ❦ "What has Mary
got that these girls haven't?" she asked with some
asperity. ❦ "Mary has patience," said the old man.

158

A FAIRY, who for appearances' sake had married a beautiful girl, discovered her being screwed by her employer on an office couch. He reported his indignation to a fairy friend. ❡ "I hope you got your revenge," said this latter. ❡ "I should say I did," the other replied. "I utterly destroyed the couch."

159

T HE train came to a halt with a sudden jar. Two men sprang into the aisles, one a tall man, the other short. Both brandished guns. "Hands up everybody," yelled the tall man. "You men line up on this side, women on the other. Now we ain't goin' to hurt nobody that behaves. Gents, shell out your dough and jewelry. All the men are goin' to be robbed and then we'll fuck all the women." ❡ "Easy now, easy," protested the smaller robber, "never mind that last. We'll just cop the dough and beat it." ❡ "You mind your own business," spoke up an old maid. "Who's robbing this train, I'd like to know."

160

A MAN accompanied a whore to her flat one night, and as she slipped into bed he asked her how much she charged. "Five dollars," said the woman. "Well," said the man, "if you'll keep both hands on the cheeks of my arse while I'm fucking you, all the time, mind you, I'll give you two dollars extra." ❡ Wondering at this vagary, the whore complied. Finished, the man pulled up his trousers and prepared

to pay her. ⟪ "Would you mind telling me," said
the woman, "just what thrill you get out of my holding
my hands that way." ⟪ "I don't get any thrill," said
the man, as he drew out a huge roll of bills, "I get
safety. For two bucks I know your hands are on my
arse, not in my pockets."

161

A NOTORIOUS cock-sucker was once caught going
down on one of the Singer midgets. His friends
ridiculed him, and asked him why he didn't pick some
one his size. Whereupon, the fairy, smiling mysterious-
ly, said, "I couldn't, you know. Doctor's orders. I'm
on a diet."

162

ONE of the parodies on the famous *Gallagher and
Shean* song is as follows:
Oh, Mr. Gallagher, oh, Mr. Gallagher,
Have you heard about the greatest sport in life?
I have often heard it said
That it's always done in bed,
And the girlie doesn't have to be your wife.
Oh, Mr. Shean, oh, Mr. Shean,
Now the way you talk you'd think that I was green.
Will you tell me what to wear
If you have a lady bare?
A jockstrop, Mr. Gallagher?
No, a condom, Mr. Shean.

163

A FOOL and her legs are soon parted.—*"Bugs" Baer.*

164

SENATOR HOARE of Massachusetts was one day delivering a long speech against a certain bill for which Senator Roscoe Conkling stood sponsor. As he outlined his points against the bill Senator Hoare kept first his right hand, and then his left in his trousers' pockets. Senator Conkling, who was a noted wit, rose to remark that 'the Senator from Massachusetts seems to be leaving no stone unturned to prevent the passage of this bill.'

165

A NEW YORK newspaper was guilty once of a similar jest, albeit unintentionally. Soldiers had raped a girl and the authorities were investigating. The headline read:

COMMISSION TO
EXAMINE PRIVATES
WILL LEAVE NO STONE UNTURNED
IN INVESTIGATION

166

A RE YOU going to send your wife to the country?"
"No, I think I'll fuck her myself."

167

A BANKER and patron of the arts recently told the following story at a dinner in his honor at the Green Room Club. ❡ It seems an upstate farmer was married to a frail, sickly woman, himself being hale and robust, as is frequently the case. It chanced that his wife fell sick and a nurse was sent for. She arrived, a blonde, big-hearted, broad-hipped Swedish girl. The farmer began to have visions. Soon these visions were realized. The nurse stayed on for several months, but finally, the wife being cured, returned to the city. ❡ Some weeks later, as the couple were at breakfast, a letter was handed to the farmer. He read it and his brow clouded. He muttered and scowled. His wife begged him to tell her what was in the letter. ❡ "Oh, it's nothing, Martha," said the farmer. ❡ "But you seem so worried," said the wife. "Remember, we are married and should be as one person in our joys and in our sorrows. We should feel together, share responsibilities together, in short be as one. Now what is troubling you?" ❡ "Well, since you put it that way," the farmer said, "this letter is from that Swedish girl. It seems she has found out she is in trouble, and she blames *us*."

168

A NOTHER and older version of this story makes the son say to his father, with whom he is in partnership: "Well, dad, since you put it that way, our stenographer is knocked up and wants *us* to marry her."

169

A GROUP of department store girls were discussing their affairs one afternoon when one of the group said to a Swedish girl, who was with them: "You know you're very foolish not to do what we're all doing. When any of these travelling men ask you to go out with them, go. Do what they tell you, and you'll get five or ten bucks maybe. That's the only way to

make some money." ❡ "Aye bane try," said the Swede.
❡ A few days later she met her friend and reported
that the scheme was not so good. "Aye ban go out with
traveller mine, like you say, und aye ban do like he
ask. In morning aye bane say, 'giff me fife dollars, or
ten maybe.' He bane say, 'go take a good shit for
yourself,' und when aye coom back, he bane gone!"

170

THE proprietor of a couple of whorehouses found
himself in need of ready cash, so he tried to raise
a loan on his property. He was refused by the first five
banks he tried. Finally the president of a small bank
seemed to think well of the collateral, and asked him,
"Are you rated?" ❡ "Oh, I'm not raided more than
once a week," was the rejoinder.

171

A CUSTOMER who ordered a condom in a drug store
was asked if he wanted one that was guaranteed.
"Sure," he answered, "but what does the guarantee do?"
❡ "Well," said the clerk, "that's to keep it from breaking within a week. Of course if it does, why, er, . .
the guarantee runs out. . . "

172

AN ENGLISHMAN returned home suddenly one day
from a meeting in the House and directed that
his wife be sent to him. ❡ "Madame is in her boudoir," the butler replied. ❡ "Very well, then, I'll go
to her," said m'Lord. ❡ "I'm afraid, Sir, she has
company," suggested the servant. ❡ True enough,

when the M.P. softly opened the the door of his wife's
bedroom he saw her, or more properly her legs, high in
the air, under the vigorous stroking of her lover. The
Englishman seized his hunting rifle from a rack and
levelled it on the offenders. ❡ "Remember, Sir, you're
a sportsman," softly whispered the butler. "Get him
on the rise."

173

Prix: What was the slipperiest day in Jerusalem?
❡ Bollix: How should I know. What was?
❡ Prix: When Balaam rode through on his ass.

174

THE old couple had just gone to bed ❡ "Nu,
Meyer, do something," prompted the old woman.
❡ "No," said Meyer, "no. Honest, Becky, I'm too
tired to think of anyone."

175

ANOTHER old couple, after an evening at a risqué
French farce, retired, and the old gentleman felt
a faint touch of the urge that had come to him but rare-
ly in his latter years. ❡ "Come on, Martha, let's have
a party," he insinuated. ❡ "Go ahead," said she.
Next morning when they woke she said to him in a tone
of interest: "How did you make out last night, John?"

176

THE two most useless things in the world, says an
Italian sage, are a man's tits and the Pope's balls.

177

A WELL-ENDOWED groom and his newly-wed bride arrived at a hotel on the first night of their honeymoon and immediately prepared for bed. "Here's where I cut the gash that never heals," said the groom in an exultant voice. "Go easy, lover, go easy, please," the bride begged. "You know I have a weak heart." "Don't you worry, honey," her husband assured her. "I'll go awful easy as I pass the heart."

178

A N ELDERLY couple attended a concert in Carnegie Hall one afternoon, and as they left the old lady asked her husband whether he had enjoyed the singing of the tenor. ⊄ "Oh, he was pretty good," said he. ⊄ "Why you poor, deaf, old dear," his wife squeaked. "He's bawls like a bull." ⊄ "He *has?*" the old man asked in wonder. ⊄ "No, dear, he *does.*"

179

A RATHER buxom woman of Slavic origin called on her family physician and startled him by asking him what was the best way to commit suicide. "Because I want to do a good job, doctor; make no fuss, or muss or nothing." ⊄ "Why, this is unusual," said the medical man. "What on earth do you want to do a thing like that for?" ⊄ "Never mind, doctor, I got plenty trouble, with my husband, trouble with money, the children. Anyway, if you don't tell me the best way I'll jump off a high building and maybe yet kill a couple innocent people, so you better tell me."

❡ "Well, if you take it that way," said he, "the best thing to do is to go home, undress, go to bed and shoot yourself about two inches below the left breast."

❡ The woman took his advice, went home and blew off her kneecap!

180

LITTLE Jimmy was discovered by his mother, behind the barn, holding one of his pet rabbits by the ears, shaking it vigorously, the while he yelled: "Two times two. Three times three. Five times four."

❡ "Why, what on earth are you doing?" his mother asked. ❡ "Teacher is a liar, ma," he said. "She told us that rabbits multiply rapidly."

181

THE REASON I don't cheat," said one married man to another, "is that I find it so hard to keep up with my legitimate screwing."

182

A YOUTH of twenty came to a whorehouse once and asked the Madam to give him a girl who had a clap. In vain that lady protested no such girls were permitted in her establishment. The young man insisted that that was the only girl he would screw. She pressed him for the reason for his strange desire.

❡ "Well, you see," he said, "I want to get it. Then I'll go home and fuck the cook. She'll give it to the ice man, he'll give it to the maid, she'll pass it to father, he'll give it to mother, and she'll give it to the new minister we've got. And that's the son-of-a-bitch I'm after!"

183

"YOU'LL never be a success as a whore," said one young woman to another. "You don't know how to get your price. The right time to ask a man for money is while he's screwing you. When his eyes get glassy ask him for ten dollars. He can't refuse you." ¶ Next day she met her friend and asked her how the idea had worked out. ¶ "Rotten," said she. "When his eyes got glassy, I went stone blind."

184

COHEN and Goldberg were partners and were quite successful, when suddenly, out of a clear sky ruin fell on them. Cohen ran about the place, tearing the hair out of his head by the handful. Goldberg, on the other hand, seemed to be more calm about it. He strutted up and down, his hands in pockets. ¶ "Bastard!" yelled Cohen. "Louse! Look how you enjoy this trouble. I'm going around tearing the hair from my head and you walk around like a sport." ¶ "Never mind, Cohen," said Goldberg, "I'm tearing my hair out too. But nobody *sees me.*"

185

A YOUNG girl who had married an old man was asked how she liked living with him. ¶ "Oh, its the same thing, weak in, weak out," she answered.

186

ANOTHER young woman for whom a marriage with an old man was being arranged by her parents refused to go through with the ceremony because, as she put it, "I don't want to feel old age creeping on me."

187

OF ANOTHER elderly gentleman approaching belated matrimony it was said: "He's so old he'll have to eat it with a spoon!"

188

AN OLD man, married to a young girl, had tried by every means in his power to consummate his marriage. His pecker simply wouldn't stand up under the duty. ⁋ Finally the girl said to him, "I guess I'll have to do a handstand and let you drop it in."

189

TWO OLD fellows were discussing their sexual prowess. ⁋ "How often do you do it, nowadays?" asked one. ⁋ Oh, tri-wekly," was the reply. ⁋ "How do you spell tri-weekly? tri- or try?"

190

AN IRISHMAN and his six children entered a crowded trolley car. There were just six seats vacant, which the children grabbed. ⁋ "Why do ye stand?" asked the conductor. "Why don't one of these boys get up and give you a seat?" ⁋ "Oh, that's all right," said the Irishman. "They're all my children, let them sit."

⊄ "Well," said the conductor, "it looks like you've fucked yourself out of a seat."

191

A YOUNG woman was being delivered of a child. Downstairs waited her Sam. Maizie suffered a great deal of pain, and, altogether, had a hard time of it. Finally, when it was all over, she sighed and said: "If this here is what married life is like, you go down and tell Sam our engagement is off!"

192

T HERE is an old Andalusian proverb which goes this way: Big woman, big cunt; little woman, *all* cunt!

193

F RED ALLEN, a 'nut' comedian, says his girl's mouth is all right, as a (w)hole.

194

B UD FISHER, the cartoonist and creator of the famous *Mutt and Jeff* series, says he hates to screw dog-fashion. "It's too lonesome. There's no one to talk to."

195

T HE OWL Drug Stores in San Francisco have a system by which any customer dissatisfied with his purchase may exchange it. Recently a woman came into one of the stores and asked for Mr. Owl. The manager, not wishing to embarrass her, said that 'Mr. Owl' was out to lunch, couldn't he, the manager, do something. "Yes," said the young lady. "Your sign says you change anything if the customer ain't satisfied. Well, I ain't, and I want you to change this whirlin' douche spray I bought last year for a couple of bottles of Mellin's baby food!"

196

A N IRISHMAN whose wife gave birth regularly, each year, was greatly troubled by this happening, as it became increasingly difficult to take care of his family. Accordingly, he asked a friend what he could do to prevent children. His friend presented him with a couple dozen condoms and told him to use them, buying more when this supply ran out. A year later he met the Irishman again, and the latter complained that his wife had again given birth to a child. ⁊ "Didn't you use those rubber protectors I gave you?" ⁊ "Sure I used them," said Pat. "And didn't I have to cut off the heads of 'em because they wouldn't fit?"

197

"M AMMA," said a little girl, "I know why daddie has such a big belly. I saw nurse blowing it up this mornnig."

198

A MARRIED man whose wife presented him with a child every year without fail, was at his wits' end for a remedy. He spoke to one of his friends who was keeping a woman. "How is it," he asked, "your girl never gets caught, while my wife has a child every year? What does that girl of yours use?" ❡ "Why, she uses Listerine," his friend replied. ❡ "Listerine? Why, that's a mouth wash," said the first. ❡ "Who says it ain't?"

199

NAT GOODWIN used to tell the story of the chap who got drunk and went to a whorehouse. He picked for his partner the dirtiest woman in the place. In fact, said this chap, relating his experience afterwards, when he woke up the next morning the only clean part of her was the teat next to him!

200

There was an old monk in Madrid,
Who cast lascivious eyes on a kid.
Said he, "Oh, what joy
To bugger that boy.
I'll do it," he said. And, by God, he did!

201

DURING the civil war a young woman and her maiden aunt were alone in their home in the South. The Yankees invaded the town and a couple of soldiers, searching for the enemy, came to the house. "We ain't goin' to harm you," said one. "All we're going to do is to give you a good fuck." ❡ The young woman began to plead for mercy, but her aunt interrupted her. "Don't holler," she said. "Them soldiers got their orders. War is war!"

202

WHEN the Kaiser's second wife left him, in a huff, the news came out that he had taken pills to give him a hard on. According to a facetious critic the medicine backfired, and he got piles!

203

A YOUNG couple on their honeymoon were travelling to Los Angeles. The train ran into trouble going through Texas and barely crawled along. ❡ "Harry dear," said the young bride, "I'm afraid if the train doesn't hurry up the intercourse season will be over by the time we arrive." ❡ "Nonsense," said her husband. "What makes you think that? Intercourse doesn't go by seasons." ❡ "Well," she naively replied, "I heard a travelling man say a while ago that if the train didn't get a move on the fucking season would be over."

204

PRIX: Why is a woman like a bank? ❡ Bollix: I don't know. Why? ❡ Prix: Because you lose all interest when you withdraw.

205

AN OLD man had a set of monkey glands installed in his system and shortly thereafter was married. In due time his wife came to labor, and the good old man waited outside the room, eagerly. Finally the doctor stuck his head outside the door and the husband besieged him. "What is it?" he begged, "a boy or a girl?" ❧ "Don't be so goddam impatient," the doctor said. "Wait till it comes down off the chandelier and I'll tell you."

206

NAT GOODWIN was fond of reciting the following limerick:
There are many fine ladies in Birmingham.
Have you heard the awful scandal concerning 'em?
How they lifted the frock
And played with the cock
Of the Bishop while he was confirming 'em.

207

"BELIEVE me, radio is a wonderful thing," said one enthusiast to a friend. "Last night I got home very late and began working the knobs of my set and in a little while I got Cuba." ❧ "That ain't nothin'," said his friend. "When I got home last night I stuck my arse out of the window and I got Chili!"

208

IT WAS said of a certain erotomaniac that he had cunt on his mind so much that regularly every month he had a nosebleed!

209

WALKING down the street a couple of fellows passed a third, a mutual acquaintance. "Do you see that guy?" asked one. "He's a horse cock." ❧ "Now, now," his friend protested, "don't call him

that. He's really a nice fellow. He's no horse cock."
❡ "Well, he'll do till one comes along, then."

210

A LAWYER will tell you the following story as a
true one. And, indeed, it is not beyond the limits
of the probable. ❡ A rape case was on the calendar
and the district attorney was examining the only one
who had witnessed the assault. He was a rather
"tough" specimen from the dregs of the city. Former
evidence had shown that this man had fallen drunk
in a tenement hallway and was roused from his stupor
by the cries of the woman. "Now, Mr. Jackson," said
the lawyer, "just tell the court what happened as you
saw it." ❡ "Well, yer honor, when I hear her a-
bawlin' I looks up and I sees first he has her skoit up,
and her big ass wuz . . ." ❡ A shudder went over the
courtroom. The judge rapped briskly on his desk.
"The witness must remember he is in the presence of
a court of justice," was the reprimand. "We want you
to tell just what you saw, but we cannot tolerate such
language in the courtroom. Now proceed with your
narrative." ❡ "Well, yer honor, I'll do the best I
can. He had one hand . . there where I told you, and
with the other he was tryin' to shut her mouth, while
all the time he was wigglin' tryin' to get his . . all
the time . . his . . he was tryin' to get his prick . . ."
❡ Another shudder went over the courtroom. Again
the judge rapped briskly. "The witness will have to
choose his language more carefully. We will not tolerate vulgarity at this bar. There are other words for
these things The next offense against the decency of

this court will be punished." ❑ Rather nonplussed, but not daunted, the fellow proceeded. "Yer honor, I've told you how he was wigglin.' But what with one hand on what I told yuh, and th' other holding her mouth shut he had nothin' to hold what I told you so's he could get it in her . . Jedge, will it please yer honor to tell me the polite word fer cunt?"

211

There was a young lady from Spain,
Whose face was exceedingly plain;
But her cunt had a pucker
That made the men fuck her,
Again, and again, and again!

212

A   TRAVELLING man who applied for a room at a
         hotel in a Western town was told that there
wasn't a single one left, except one that had the reputation of being haunted. ❑ "That's bull," he said.
"There ain't any such thing as ghosts; besides, I ain't
afraid of them, if there are. I'll take the room."
❑ "But this is no ordinary ghost," mine host said,
winking to the clerk. "The last five men who slept in
that room saw the ghost and got chollyrobus, and next
morning we found them dead." ❑ "What's chollyrobus?" asked the traveller. ❑ "Why, the sight of
the spirit made them shit out their guts," said the Land-
lord. ❑ But the traveller would not be dismayed and
insisted on taking the room. To test his nerve the hotel
man took the entrails of a freshly killed chicken, and
stealing softly to the haunted room deposited them in

the guest's bed, between his thighs and well up near the anus. When the traveller came down next morning he was asked how he had slept, and whether the ghost had visited him. ❡ "No," he said, "I didn't see any ghost. But I got that chollyrobus you spoke about. When I woke up, there lay my guts in bed. But with the help of a little vaseline I got them all back!"

213

"**P**HWAT are ye eatin' all them onions fer, buddy?" Pat asked one of the other ditch diggers. "Onions good. Grow hair on da chest," was the reply. "Thin phwhy not eat beans, they blow 'em off yer arsehole!"

214

AS THE waitress came near the patron he blew a noisy fart. "Don't be alarmed," he said. "That's only A. S. S. broadcasting." ❡ "Oh," said the girl, "from the smell I thought it was B. V. D. receiving."

215

A BUSINESS man whose wife had been running about with many men determined to bring matters to a head, so he wrote the following letter to Mr. Brown: "My dear Sir: I am fully aware of your relations with my wife. Be at my office at 2 o'clock sharp on Monday. Yours truly, H. Smith." ❡ Brown, when he received the letter, called in his stenographer. "Mary," he said, "take this down: My dear Smith: Your circular letter received. Will attend conference on time."

216

"CAN PAPA eat glass?" asked Tommy of his mother. ℂ "Why no," she answered. "What makes you think so?" ℂ "Well, I just heard him tell nurse that if she'd put out the light he'd eat it."

217

MABLE and Jack came in late one Saturday night from "Tex's." They had had a little "tiff" early in the evening, and its effect still lingered. Jack was good-humored, and had not taken the disagreement seriously. Mable, however, still persisted in remaining cold. Getting far over on her side of the bed, she settled herself at once for sleep. Jack, as was his custom, adjusted his lamp and began his bed-time reading. He had been reading quietly for some time when she felt his hand on her belly, then on her hip, then on her groin. But when his fingers were dangerously near her placket she turned on him suddenly and glared angrily. ℂ "Oh, don't worry, heart's delight. I was only going to wet my finger to turn the page."

218

THE little bank clerk was very anxious to dandle an heir on his arm. But he had been married three years, had never used a contraceptive, and still his wife showed no signs of the tumor which subsides automatically in nine months. "What can I do?" he inquired of a husky friend who was the father of three strapping boys. "I've done it to her in every way those French books of yours show. I've done it to her at all times of the month. And still she's as flat as a pancake." ❡ His friend was wearied by his story. "I'll tell you, Jim, a sure way we can get her pregnant," he said, firmly. ❡ The little man jumped at it immediately. "For heaven's sake let's hear." ❡ You send her down to the sea for two months. You know it's often the woman's fault,—run-down condition, colds, and so forth. You send her where she'll get built up, get sunshine every day, fresh air, ten hours of undisturbed sleep every night, lots of food, eggs and fish, and the like. When she's all rested up and just can't hold herself to get back to you, send for her, get her all washed up at a Turkish bath, then, Jim, *send for me!*"

219

THE poor young man had eloped with the rich man's daughter. After the perfunctory formality at City Hall they had hurried to a half-furnished, one-room apartment that went by the name of a studio in Greenwich Village. It was evening when they emerged from their first delerium together. ❡ "What shall we call it, dearest?" whispered the girl, whose instincts were healthy enough, though a little too pink with romanticism. ❡ "Well, if he gets out of that," said he, throwing the condom out of the window, "we'll name him Houdini."

220

THE food in the *Blue Star* lunch room was terrible, and the customer called the waiter to him. "Do me a favor," he asked. "Promise me you'll do just what I tell you. Take this steak right back to the chef and tell him to stick it up his arse. Now remember, do just what I told you." ❡ The waiter promised, and bore off the order. When he returned the customer called him again and asked if he had delivered the message. ❡ "The chef said you'll have to take your turn," the waiter answered; "there's a beef stew and a cocoanut pie ahead of you."

221

"WHAT's Gerty Brown doing now? I hear she was down and out." ❡ "Oh, no, Gerty's all right now. You see she's taken it into her head to make a living."

222

GEORGE BROWN, very horny, was walking down Broadway with his Sophie. George was manoeuvring her to a hotel, where he could screw the young lady to his heart's content, and, he was little bit impatient to get there. They were passing a jewelry store. Sophie dragged him to the window. "I like that wrist watch," she said. "All right," George answered. "I'll get it for you. Come on." They walked on, till they passed a tailor's shop. "Buy me that dress," Sophie wheedled. "Sure," said George. "Come on." Next they passed a novelty store. "Get me that pocketbook," Sophie declared, and again George promised he would, and hurried her along to the hotel. There he satisfied himself deliriously, and they began the journey home. As they passed the novelty store she tried to drag him inside for the pocketbook, but he pulled her away. Next they came to the tailor's, and again he drew her away from the window. As they passed the jewelry store Sophie said to him, "Come

on inside and get me that wrist watch." "Huh-uh," said
George. "When I'm hard, I'm soft, but when I'm soft, I'm
hard."

223

THE twins were having a bath and both parents
watched, fondly. Suddenly Mary began to cry.
"Mamma," I want one of those things that's hanging
from Bobby," pointing to his little pecker. ⊄ "Quiet,
now, quiet," mother said. "If you're a good little girl
you'll get one of them." ⊄ "And if you're a bad little
girl," said father, "you'll get a lot of them."

224

THE shortest fairy tale in the world: "Leggo my
ears, I know my business."

225

THE dirtiest story ever told, in my opinion, is the
one about the boy who was screwing his mother
when she said, "My, Jimmy, your prick is bigger than
dad's."

226

RABINOWITZ made a lot of money in the war and
his wife spent some of it for clothes. He came
home one evening to find her gorgeously arrayed in a
low-cut evening gown. ⊄ "My, how nice you look!"
he said. "What's this lovely thing on the end here?"

¶ "That's lace," his wife replied. ¶ "How nice your titties look under it," Rabinowitz went on. "And ooh, your shape, its grand! What makes that?" ¶ "Oh, that's a new corset I got today," she replied. ¶ Her husband stood off a ways to admire her. Suddenly he said, "Becky, your pants are coming down!" ¶ Alarmed, she surveyed herself in the mirror, but everything seemed to her to be in shape. "Go on, you fool," she said, "they ain't." ¶ "Becky, I tell you your pants are coming down," her husband insisted. ¶ Again she looked, and again reassured herself. ¶ "They ain't" she said. ¶ "Becky," her husband answered, "I made up my mind!"

227

THE trouble with you," said a man in the audience to a public speaker, "is that you have a diarrhea of words and a constipation of ideas."

228

A FARMER once wrote to Sears Roebuck & Company to ask for the price of toilet paper. He received an answer directing him to look on page 307 of their catalogue. ¶ "If I had your catalogue," he wrote back, "would I ask you for the price of toilet paper?"

229

A TALL southerner, of some heft, registered with a gal at a dingy hotel in the Bottoms of Kansas City, and after retiring with her, went down to the lobby of the hotel to smoke a huge cigar. The bellboy, passing his room, heard moans, and softly opened the door. The lady lay naked on the bed, writhing and moaning, her eyes narrowing and dilating as she heaved and tossed, in the motions of a good screwing. The bellhop hurried down and approached the big fella. "Say," he said, "your gal is layin' on the bed, movin' around like someone's on her. Ain't you 'fraid some- one might cop her out?" "No sir-ee, sonny!" said the big stud. "When ah fucks 'em, they stays fucked!"

230

UP IN New Haven there was a girl nearly every senior in the college had screwed. They were sur- prised one day when she told them she was to be mar- ried to a grocer. A party of the students gathered, after midnight, at the Taft, in the hallway outside the room of the honeymooning young couple. One of the seniors was hoisted so he could look over the transom and report to the others, who were strung out in a long line to the elevators. ⟨ "He's kissing her now," the lookout reported. Down the corridor rang the phrase, "He's kissing her." ⟨ "Now he's taking off her clothes," came the report, to be repeated, in a whisper, "He's taking off her clothes. . ." "He's taking off her clothes. . ." "He's taking off her clothes." Again the watcher reported, "He's kissing her titties." And down the corridor the information flew. "They've got into bed." "They're in bed," was the whisper, to be re- peated down the line. ⟨ Suddenly the lookout heard the girl say to her husband, "Oh, you're putting it where no man had it before!" The peeper reported to his fellows, "He's fucking her in the ass." "He's fucking her in the arse. . ." "He's fucking her in the arse. . ."

231

"I'VE JUST returned from a visit to Cedar Rapids, my home town," said a prominent cartoonist to a friend of his, in the *Friar's Club*. "You know its a funny thing, but the population of that town hasn't increased or decreased in twenty years. But I know the reason. Every time a child is born there, some one leaves town!"

232

DURING the recent coal shortage, when the population of New York had its fuel rationed to it, a coal dealer sent one of his truckmen with a load of hard and soft coal up to his house in the suburbs, with instructions to dump both loads in his cellar, in different corners. The coal man's wife was glad to receive the coal, but after he had finished loading the soft into the cellar she was suddenly called away to town, and shut up her house. ❡ The truckman, unable to release the rest of the coal, wired to his employer as follows: "Dropped one load. Got my hard on. She has it closed so I can't put it in!"

233

A COUPLE, childless after ten years of married life, visited a physician for the purpose of determining whose fault it was. The doctor told the husband that he was sterile, and that if they really desired a child it would be necessary for some other man to impregnate the wife. After they left, the couple talked it over, and, so great was their desire to have a child, the husband agreed to let another man stay with his wife. ❡ They went to another city, so they would not be known, and while the woman waited in her room, her husband approached a strong-looking man and said to him, "Say, I know where you can get a fine piece of tail. Go up to room 425. There's a swell looking dame there who's crazy for a screw." ❡ The stranger thanked him and made for the elevator at once. After a time he returned, and the husband, who had suffered every agony, but had stifled it with the joyful thought of the child that was to be theirs, came up to his proxy. ❡ "Well, how did you like her?" "Fine," replied the stranger. "Best screw I've had in years. But I couldn't overcome the fear that she might not be all right, so I used a condom."

234

A MIDGET, billed to appear at a local vaudeville theatre, failed to put in an appearance at the Monday matinée. The manager explained to his friends that the midget had been arrested, *'for going up on a woman.'*

235

S ILVERMAN was making his first road trip, as far as Chicago. His friend, Weinstein, told him what a wonderful town the Windy City is, and recounted his many experiences with women in Lincoln Park, on the Loop and the Boulevard. "It's the greatest town in the world for tail," he told Silverman. ❡ The latter was therefore keyed up in anticipation of the pleasures that were to be his when he arrived at the Dearborn street terminal several nights later. He went at once to a hotel, where, because there were a few conventions

in town, he could not get a room, but was told he could
sleep on a billiard table if he chose. Because it was so
late, Silverman accepted, and at once repaired to his
couch, so as to rise fresh and ready for his foray on
the city's wild women. ❡ The hotel porter, finishing
his work, lay down on the same table as Silverman, but
was shortly awakened by the latter's screaming, "Hurray fer Chicago. Hurray fer Chicago!" ❡ The porter
shook the sleeper till he woke. "Listen," he said, "holler 'hurray fer Chicago' all you like, but leave my cock
alone."

236

A MIDDLE-AGED Jewess had been a widow only a
a week when her Irish neighbor stopped her on
the street. "Why, Mrs. Cohen, it's you I see, is it?
You do be all dressed up fit to kill. Sich gay feathers,
and your Sammy's been only dead a week." ❡ "Vell,
Mrs. O'Randy, I vill haf you know mine pants is black.
Und it's dere vere I feels it most."

237

THE telephone in the gas company's office jangled.
A frantic woman's voice complained to the clerk:
"My gas is out. I've had to use a candle for two days.
Send a man up right away!"

238

TWO fellows were bragging about the size of their
pricks. Said one: "Boy, I was once in swimmin' in
the East River, and I got to thinkin' of my gal, and my jock

grew so big it stuck in the mud. Then I turned on my back to float and couldn't get past the Brooklyn Bridge!" The other scoffed. "You call that big, man? Why, when I was up in Alaska once I took out my jock to pee, and I got to thinkin' of my gal, and it got so big I couldn't put it back in my pants, and it was so cold up there in Alaska that I began to rub the root of my dick with snow to keep it from freezin', and what I couldn't reach with my hands, man, I threw snowballs at!"

239

A DOG's idea of heaven: A mile of trees and a bellyfull of piss.

240

A STRANGER sauntered up to the bar of a wildwestern saloon and asked where the toilet was. "Outside," said the barkeeper. "You'll see a pile, and that's it." ❡ The stranger went out, but in a few minutes there was a terrific din, as if the whole town was being shot up, and the stranger came dashing back into the saloon, holding up his pants with one hand, and yelling. ❡ "What the hell's the matter?" said the man behind the bar. ❡ "I don't know," said the other. "Just as I let down my pants some one took a shot at me." ❡ "Where did you let down your pants?" the bartender asked. ❡ "Outside," said the stranger. "There were two piles, not one, like you said, and I squatted over the little one." ❡ "No wonder you were shot at," said the bartender. "The little pile's the *ladies'* toilet!"

GULLIVER had been captured by the Lilliputians, and the King, to make a royal holiday, ordered his army to jack-off the giant. Thousands of soldiers took their stand along the tremendous priapus of Gulliver and began a rhythmic motion of frictioning it. For three hours they toiled, yet not one drop of sperm rewarded their efforts. ⬛ In a fury the King rode up to the Fifth Lancers, who, situated midway, were resting, apparently, and demanded to know what was wrong. "I don't know, Sire," the Captain replied. "It passed us an hour ago!"

241

RAMSEY and Lily were just married, and hastened to their rooms. A party of their friends, determined that the young couple should have neither leisure nor rest that first night, undertook to serenade them. Beneath the windows of the couple this party gathered, and at frequent intervals made the night full with their noises. Each time Ramsey essayed to draw apart the veil that kept his bride from becoming his wife, a fearful din would set in, so that he thought surely his friends were going to break into their privacy, and perhaps, catch him in the very act. Finally Lily could stand it no longer, to hover thus between the single and the married state, so she called out in peevish accents to her husband that he demand his friends to desist. He tried again and again, but they would not heed him. Finally, Lily yelled at him, "Ramsey, pee on 'em, Ramsey." The latter turned a reproachful, yet gentle look on his bride. "Honey, where do you think they are, anyway? On the roof across the street?"

242

A MIDDLE-AGED gentleman, a widower, married again. On his wedding night, to please his bride who was much younger than he, he had endeavored to excel all his past efforts. ❰ In the morning, as he was about to apologize, she said to him, "Dear, I must apologize to you. I neglected to tell you before our marriage that I have asthma. It must have bothered you last night." ❰ "Oh," said her husband, greatly relieved; "is that what it was? I thought you were hissing me!"

243

A N ACTOR, who endeavored to emulate in a matrimonial way the late Nat Goodwin, had recently been married to his fifth wife. A friend who met him at the Lambs' Club asked him how he liked his new wife. ❰ "Oh, she's all right," the actor replied. "But she has no conception of the part."

244

A YOUNG couple had registered at a hotel and were snugly ensconced under the sheets, with the lights out, when the man complained that the girl was too tight for him. ❰ "I haven't been stayed with in a long time," she answered. "But if you'll look in the bag on the dresser you'll find a tube of vaseline. Rub it on the head and it'll slip in easy." ❰ Her partner reached out in the dark, got the tube, and followed instructions, with satisfactory results. ❰ Next morning, however, he was startled to observe that the head had fallen off his penis. ❑ "What the hell is this? Did you bite this off?" he roared. The lady gazed a moment at him in perplexity. Then she burst out, "My Gawd, you must of used my *corn cure!*"

245

B IG MARK had come home drunk every Saturday night for the last two months. Linda, his strong-armed and strong-minded woman, was good and tired of it. When next Saturday came and her fella was not home at nine o'clock she locked the door and went to bed. She tossed, and had not yet fallen asleep when she heard a dull thumping on the door. "Linda, honey," came Mark's wheedling voice, "how come you've locked me out?" "I'm sick and tired of these here drunken sprees of yours, Mark Brown," she said. "I've concluded that, if you can't come to your wife sober, you can't come at all." Mark continued to thump the door. "Oh, Linda, honey, ain't you gonna let me in? I'm not stewed! Honest I ain't." "Huh! Ain't stewed! Man, I know you by now. You go and sleep off your drunk somewhere else." Mark kept on knocking. "Honest I ain't, Linda. Can't you hear me knocking? If I was stewed, do you suppose I could knock like this?" "Go on away, and lemme be." "Linda, I know you'd let me in if you knew what I'm knocking with." At this, his wife rose with alacrity and unlocked the door. Mark came in, absolutely sober, and handed her the box of candy he had brought as a peace offering. Next morning Linda was hauled into court for beating her man into insensibility.

246

THE poker game had gone steadily worse for the little drummer. He had been "low man" straight running for the last two hours. Finally he threw the cards down in disgust and took a seat over in a corner by himself. From there he was languidly watching the others play and listening to their chatter. ❡ "You know," one travelling-man was saying, "it's a funny thing, but every time I go out I have to kiss my wife goodbye on a dimple she has in her chin. Don't you think that's funny, Bill, not to be satisfied unless I kiss her there?" ❡ "Why no," said Bill. "My wife's got a funnier one than that. Everytime I start out, I've got to kiss my wife on her titties, or I'm a brute." ❡ "Not so bad," said the fellow who was winning. "I'm lucky at cards. But I get hell when I leave home if I don't kiss my wife on the navel." ❡ "Well, I guess I'm 'low man' again," said the little drummer in the corner. "Good night."

247

THE pastor of the Baptist church in a little Indiana town was speaking a few words on proper conduct to the Sunday school. "Now, children, before I close the lesson, I want to ask a few questions on the things I have been talking about. Willie," he said to a model little boy in the front row, "tell me, do you know where little boys and girls go when they do bad things?" ❡ "Sure," piped up the town terror, whose name was also Willie, and who had for the first time been lured into the church. "Back of the churchyard."

248

A s they danced about in the Slip Lip tea room Suzie Jackson felt something hard in Sam Brown's trousers, pressing against her. It seemed quite the longest, hardest object she had ever felt pressed against her. So she did not demur when Sam suggested they adjourn to a private room for a little session. Alone together, when she had removed her outer garments, Sam took off his coat, and, slipping his hand inside his trousers, took out a broom handle, which he laid carefully to one side. "See here," said Suzie. "I thought that was your prick." "No, ma'am," said Sam. "That's my decoy."

249

W hich brings us to the story of the fella whose penis was so large that no women who knew him would accommodate him. None dared. Finally, in desperation he took a friend's advice and picked up a woman who was not aware of his *elephantiasis,* and, in a dark room, rammed his weapon home. The lady groaned loudly. Then in a determined voice cried out, *"You* can stay, but your friend has *got to go!"*

250

T hree times the beautiful lady had stared invitingingly at a man who wandered back and forth in the lobby of the Ritz. Finally she grew bolder, although she had received no encouragement, and approached him. "Hello," she said, with a smile. ❡ "Don't bother, madam," said the man. "Liquor is my weakness."

251

COHEN had submitted a sample of his urine to the doctor and eagerly awaited the analysis. "It is sixty-five per cent sugar and thirty-five per cent albumen," he was informed. ❡ "Ain't there no piss in it, doctor?" Cohen asked.

252

A TRAVELLING man was taking leave of his sweetie. As a last favor he begged her to have her private parts photographed. ❡ "Why?" she asked. ❡ "So when I get on the road, and feel lonesome, I can look at the picture and remain true to you," he answered. "All right," said the girl. "But you must have a photograph made of your prick." ❡ "Why?" it was his turn to ask. ❡ "So I can have it enlarged," answered the girl.

253

A BEAUTIFUL brunette was delivered of a fine-looking baby in a maternity hospital, only,—the infant had red hair. ❡ "Ah," said the doctor, smiling, "father red-headed?" ❡ "I don't know," said the brunette. "He kept his hat on."

254

IT WAS a foggy morning, and the fishing smacks off Gloucester nosed their way out of the harbor. Suddenly a sailor in one hailed another: "Hello, John, I have news for ye." ❡ "What is it?" ❡ "Wife had a baby, a boy." ❡ "What'd he weight?" the other voice called. ⟪ " Four pounds," came the reply, thru the fog. ⟪ "Hell, you hardly got your bait back!"

255

GENTLEMEN, it is our pleasure to announce to you that Mr. Al Smith has accepted the nomination as Democratic candidate for the President of the United States. We have no doubt he will pull the votes of the country's entire male population. We are planning an extensive campaign, and every State will in a few days be flooded with the slogan,

VOTE FOR AL SMITH
AND HAVE YOUR WET DREAMS COME TRUE.

256

IT WAS their first Sunday afternoon drive after their engagement. He had been watching for a "comfort station" for the last twenty-five miles. It was a lonely, hilly road with this refinement of civilization few and far between. Fearing he would not be able to contain himself any longer, he stopped the car, excused himself, and clambered down a steep embankment. When he believed he was safely out of hearing and sight he hurriedly bared his bottom, squatted, and released the anal sphincter. ⟪ "Who's here!" came a threatening voice from just below him. ⟪ "Ssh, ssh, I got my girl with me." ⟪ "What the hell you think I got, a duck?"

257

SHE'S got an elevator cunt—always room for one more.

258

Visiting a red-light district of town, a travelling man accosted a neat looking wench and asked her what she charged. "My charges," said the girl, "is one dollar, two, and five dollars." "Why the different prices?" the horny stranger asked. "Well," said the woman, "for one dollar you get a straight fuck. For two dollars I also fucks. But for five dollars, I make a perfect fool of myself."

259

A buyer from Toledo arrived one day in New York, and, after visiting one of the firms with which he did business, asked the salesman to tell him where he could pick up a dame. "Go up to 42nd Street and Broadway," said the salesman, "and you can have the pick of New York. Take the subway up." ❡ The buyer did as he was told, but fell asleep and woke up at 72nd Street instead. Here, however, he was immediately successful. A fine looking woman passed. He tipped his hat, to her. She acknowledged his greeting. The acquaintance and understanding were quickly made, and the woman invited the buyer to her house. "My husband said he wouldn't be home tonight, so we can go out together for a good time," she said. ❡ However, they were no sooner in the flat, and the woman had just managed to slip off her dress, when they heard the scraping of a key in the lock. "Quick," my husband, whispered the lady. "Get in the next room on that ladder and make believe you are fixing that clock on the wall." ❡ The buyer did as he was told. In the next room he heard voices. "Hello, honey," said a

man's deep voice. "I found I didn't have to stay down-
town after all. Who's in the next room?" ❡ "Oh,
that's only the man to fix the clock," said the woman's
voice. Obediently the buyer turned the handles so the
clock struck. ❡ The door was opened, and a voice
cried out, "You son-of-a-bitch, I told you to go to
42nd Street!"

260

A N ELEVATOR man, remarked Silas Crapp, is the only
person who can go down and whistle at the same
time.

261

F ROM his vantage point in the upper berth the travelling man was watching a lady in the berth below
prepare for rest. First she unscrewed a pair of false
breasts. Then she removed a wig. Next she unscrewed
a false eye, and was in the midst of unscrewing an arti-
ficial limb when she spied the peeper. ❡ "What are
you looking at?" she shrilled. "What do you want?"
❡ "You know damn well what I want," was the reply.
"Unscrew it and throw it up here."

262

T WO married men met on the street. One, a timorous
fellow, said to the other, "Do you cheat?"
❡ "Sure," was the reply. ❡ The shy one looked at
his friend with envy. "Don't your conscience bother
you?" he asked. ❡ "Yes, for nine days. After that if
everything is all right. . . ."

263

AFTER having been stared at for some five minutes, the pretty young woman went up to the fresh man and said, "What are you looking at me like that for?" ❡ "Well, Miss," said he, "if I had a cock eye you'd be the mother of four children by now."

264

THERE was a curious sight on Broadway one day last week. A Scotchman was observed, riding up and down the White Way, on a horse. But Sandy, instead of facing front had seated himself so that he faced the horse's tail. Careful questioning elicited the information that the Scot had dropped a dime in the oats that morning.

265

AN IRISHMAN and an Italian were working on a sewer full of crap. The Irishman was up to his knees in the muck, handing it up by the bucketfuls to the Italian, clean and dry above. One of Pat's friends remonstrated with him. Why didn't he send the guy down into the mire and pick the easy job himself? "Na," said Pat. "No Italian can hand me shit!"

266

A NOTORIOUS whore suddenly got religion and became a Salvation Army convert. At an experience meeting she was relating the details of her conversion, while her former crony sat in the auditorium and listened. ❡ "Before I saw the light," said the glorified whore, "I lay in the arms of many men. I lay in the arms of sailors, soldiers, civilians, doctors, merchants, lawyers. But now, my friends, that I have lain in the arms of Jesus..." ❡ "That's right, kid," her friend interrupted. "Fuck 'em all!"

267

A VARIANT of the above story has for its hero a tough British soldier who was the terror of the army. Two shells fell on either side of him, one day at Gallipoli, without inflicting on him so much as a scratch. So he embraced the true Lord. At a meeting of soldiers, welfare workers, and Red Cross nurses, back of the lines, he was telling his experiences. Concluding his remarks he said: "See these fine shoes? Christ gave me those. See these fine breeches? Christ gave me those. See this elegant weskit? This top hat? Christ gave me those. What did the devil ever give me? Narthin'. *Fuck* the devil!"

268

"D O YOU like cocktails?" asked the college boy of the shy young lady, in a restaurant. ❡ "Oh, yes. Tell me some!"

269

I T WAS a school in the farming district, and one morning Johnny came late. "Johnny, why are you late today?" teacher asked. ❡ "This morning I had to bring the bull out to the cow, teacher." ❡ "That's no excuse," said the lady. "Couldn't your father do that?"

❡ "No, teacher," said Johnny. "You got to have the bull!"

270

A FELLOW excitedly entered a noted surgeon's office. "Doctor," he panted, "I want you to castrate me." "What?" marvelled the medico. "A husky like yourself?" "Don't ask no questions, Doc," the man responded. "Castrate me. Here's the money." Shrugging his shoulders, the doctor called his assistant, who administered ether, and the fellow lost the power of his sex. As he came out of the ether the doctor leaned over to him and said: "Now that you've had this done, and while you're on the table, why not be circumcised?" "Doggone, Doc," said the chap in a squeaky voice, "that's the word I wanted. That's what I want done!"

271

A NOTHER fella said he liked screwing a mule all right. "Only you got to go such a long way round to kiss her," he objected.

272

A DINER in the Hunting Room at the Astor who had need to go to the lavatory, was greatly disturbed to discover therein a man in evening dress, masturbating himself with great vigor. ❡ "Here, here," he expostulated, "what are you doing, man!" ❡ "Don't interrupt me," said the other, "I'm a Christian Scientist, and I'm screwing a girl in Toledo."

273

A LADY approached the paying teller's window, in a western bank. "How much are fifty thousand rubles?" she enquired. "Oh, about fifty cents," said the teller casually. "And I bought the son-of-a-bitch his breakfast!" said the lady as she walked away.

274

E AGER TO "change his luck" a man approached a prostitute. "I charge two dollars," said the woman. "You're crazy!" said the man. "I won't pay that." "All right, man, I do need the money, so I'll do it for a dollar," agreed the girl. But again he refused. "Well, then," said the prostitute, "you can have it for fifty cents, but at fifty cents, I'm losin' money!"

275

A LL THE dinner guests were assembled, having given up expecting Dr. Blank, a well-known surgeon, who was late, to say the least. However, he arrived at just that moment, breathless. Making his apologies to the hostess he explained that he had been hurriedly summoned to the hospital to perform an operation. Instantly the guests were eager to learn what the operation was, et cetera, et cetera. But the surgeon said the subject was a delicate one, what with the presence of so many ladies. ⟨ This objection was quickly over-ruled by the ladies themselves, who pointed out that since all present were married folk there should be no undue modesty. ⟨ "Well, then," said the doctor, "we cut through the penis of the patient, who was suffering from . . " ❡ "Pardon me," interrupted the hostess, "did you have to saw through the bone?" ❡ As one person the assembled company rose and bowed elaborately to the host!

276

A LONDON cabby was arrested for using abusive language to a woman passenger. The court was reproving him: "Don't you know any better than to use such language to a lady?" said the judge. ❡ "She's no lady," said the cabby. ❡ "Indeed!" said the judge. "And would you recognize a lady if you saw one?" ❡ "That I would, yer wushup," was the reply. "I had a lady fare only last week. I drives 'er from Trafalgar Square to 'er 'ouse about four mile distant and she gives me a guinea. 'Pardon, lady, yer change,' says I. But she says, 'Stick the change up yer arse.' That's what I calls a lady, yer wushup."

277

THEY were celebrating their golden wedding anniversary and the old man, in a brave and debonair moment decided he would give his wife lasting proof of his affection. When they were alone at last, and in bed, he intimated to her that he would again attempt to satisfy her, with somewhat the vigor of his youth. As she lay before him invitingly, more or less, he attempted to induce an erection. In vain he thought of Jessie Reed, Eva Brady, and other passion-provoking Follies beauties. In vain he manipulated his withered organ. He might be interested, but the man below was not.

◖ At last he shook his head sorrowfully and said, "Fifty years ago, Becky, you was ashamed. Tonight, I'm ashamed'"

278

THE waitress in a one-armed beanery determined to have some fun with a patron whose custom it was to study the menu carefully every day, and then order ham and eggs. So one day she drew a line through his favorite dish, and when he pored over the card she said to him, "Did you notice, sir, I scratched something you like?" ◖ Without looking up the customer replied, "Go wash your hands and bring me some ham and eggs."

279

AN OLD couple had gone to bed. The old man felt in himself one last spark of virility and began to toy with his spouse. He succeeded in working her up to a fervid pitch of anticipation. As he was about to inject the tip of his feebly erect ambassador his wife whispered to him hoarsely, "Meyer, reach over to the dresser for my false teeth. I want to bite you!"

280

TWO meticiously immaculate spinsters rode through the country in their Pierce Arrow, driven by their handsome chauffeur as they liked to be driven, at sixty miles an hour. At a sudden turn he ran straight into the rear end of a stray cow, and sent its members flying. He had seen it in time to prevent a serious acci-

dent, and immediately jumped out to see what harm
had been done. The old girls were considerable shaken
up. When they came to, one found a long cylindrical
hunk of the cow's udder in her lap. Taking it up af-
fectionately, she cried piteously, "Great heavens, Zeb-
bie, the chauffeur's been killed!"

281

A N UNDERSIZED fellow was on trial for rape. His ac-
cuser sat in a chair on the stand and testified that on a
summer's day he had come across her in the woods, backed
her against a tree and raped her. There was no sympathy for
the little chap. His goose was cooked. The judge ordered the
woman to step up onto the stand. As she rose it was evident
that she was several heads taller than the defendant. "How
comes it," asked the judge, "that a little bit of a fellow like
that was able to attack a large woman like yourself? It seems
to me that standing against a tree, as you say you were, he
could barely reach you." "Well, judge," admitted the plain-
tiff, "I'll admit I did stoop a little!"

282

T HE sap of the office was about to be married and
the whole staff looked forward to the event. It
came, and the morning after the sap was greeted by a
lot of knowing winks. To his confidant, however, he
admitted that he had made no attempt on his wife.
Next day he again said he had not stayed with his
spouse, and again the next. Finally, after a week or
so of married life he came in one morning, jubilant.
❡ "Gee," he told his friend, "I had a fine screw last

night!" ❡ "Why the hell did you wait all this time?" his *bon vivant* asked. "Why didn't you screw your wife the first night?" ❡ "I didn't know then that she was hump!"

283

THE young man sat on the sofa, his sweetheart in his lap. In a few days they were to be married. She was cuddling to him closely, when he spied the cat toying with a tassel at one end of the sofa. ❡ "Look, look, sweetheart," he said, banteringly, "in a couple days you'll be doing to me like the cat is doing." ❡ When the young woman turned to observe the feline, that creature was calmly licking its arse!

284

A FAIR-HAIRED man who had been away a long time, returned to find his blonde wife had been delivered of a child. His joy, however, was marred when he observed that the infant had a decided brunette cast. "Hah," he said, "how is this, the baby looks dark?" "Well, you see," said his wife, "while you was away, and I was pregnant, I was crossing a field and a feller chased me. I was so scared that it had a terrible effect on the child." "A feller chased you?" said the husband bitterly. "It looks to me like he caught you!"

285

TWO travelers reached a Western city and tried to put up at the only hotel. The proprietor informed them that there wasn't a room to be had. As they turned away in despair, however, he suggested this alternative to them. "One of you guys can come to my room. I think I'll be able to give you a shakedown there. The other go up to room 33. There's two beds in that room. In one there is a dame. But there's a screen around her bed. Just you crawl into the other one and she won't mind. ❡ His offer was accepted eagerly. But in a few minutes the man who went to room 33 returned in great agitation. "Good Christ," he said, "that woman in the other bed is dead!" ❡ "I know," said mine host. "But how the hell did you find out?"

286

BOTH partners in a jewelry concern had been screwing the stenographer when, to their consternation, they discovered she was pregnant. In their fright each tried to lay the onus of parenthood on the other. Finally one of the partners, who was in charge of out-of-town sales, went on the road. In a few weeks the stenographer was confined. ❡ The partner at home immediately wired to the one on the road: "Gertie gave birth to twins. Mine died!"

287

YOUNG Barton was away from home, visiting relatives. A woman accosted him on the streets and took him to her flat. It was the first time young Barton had ever yielded to the flesh. For several hours the woman gave him of her best. Finally, inert, he asked her how much he owed her. "Oh, give me what you think it was worth," said she, carelessly. The youth took out a swollen pocketbook and deposited its entire contents on the dresser. "Here's eighty-seven dollars," he said. "That's all the money I have with me now. I'll send you the rest later!"

288

SIMPKINS was at last persuaded to part with his virginity. It was not without some trepidation that he ventured into a bawdy house, where Fat Lizzy took ample care of him. As he emerged he said to his friend, who had brought him to the house of pleasure: "Do I like it? It was great. Say, bo, I'm going to make a hobby of this!"

289

JONES: "I was calling on a friend of mine. He was shaving himself with a tremendous big razor. 'Hell,' I said, 'that's the smallest razor you've got?' 'Naw,' says he, 'I got 'em smaller.' And then he showed me a littler one, and a littler one than that. And then he said: 'Wanna see my baby razor?' 'Sure,' I said. He goes to the door and hollers, 'O Maw, come up!' "

290

PERKINS had married the widow of a golf player. The first night, after the ceremony, they repaired to their bed and Perkins tore off a vigorous piece. Weary and satisfied, he was about to turn over to sleep, when the former widow said, "What, tired already? My first husband was never satisfied with one." Rousing himself, Perkins again entered the holy precincts,

and again attempted to turn over. "What," said the
new wife, "only twice? My last husband was never
satisfied with two in a night." Summoning all his re-
sources, Perkins again scoured her vessel. And again
he attempted to desert Aphrodite for Morpheus.
"What," said his wife, "only three times? My first
husband never neglected me so. Come on, again."
℟ Perkins turned to her and said, "now tell me, once
and for all, what's par for your hole?"

291

THE author of several current "best-sellers" in the
flippant vein is fond of the story which illustrates
the blasé nature of the Englishman. ℟ An English
House of Lords, asked "What are you doing?"
℟ "Can't you see I'm being sucked off?" said the other
Lord. ℟ "Oh, to be sure," was the reply. "By the
way, are you going to Lady Cunard's reception?"
"By all means, I wouldn't miss it for worlds." ℟ "Beg
pardon," interrupted the fairy, "I believe your Lord-
ship's come." ℟ "So I have, so I have. Here's a shill-
ing for you, my good man."

292

A YOUNG man met a chorus girl friend of his on
Broadway and tried to make the grade. "No,
sir," said she, "you can't screw me unless you pay me
five dollars." ℟ "Five bucks! Yer crazy," said the
youth. "I'd rather give up fucking." ℟ "I'd rather
sew it up," said the girl, "than do it for less." ℟ "Well,
a couple of stitches wouldn't hurt it," he said.

293

Mrs. Goldberg greeted her husband with tears when he arrived after a hard day in the shop. "Doctor Cohen says I got tuberculosis and must die yet," she moaned. ❦ "What!" shouted Goldberg, "that loafer told a big, fat woman like you that you got T.B.? I'll run see him right away." ❦ He rushed to the doctor's office and burst in on him. "Doctor Cohen," he said, "what do you mean by telling my wife she's got tuberculosis and must die? I'm Goldberg." ❦ The physician looked him over slowly, then said, "I never told your wife that. What I said was that she's got too big a tokus and must go on a diet."

294

An English landowner was showing a friend over his grounds. They came to the garden where a beautiful hedge of rose bushes were growing. ❦ "I can't understand it," said his friend. "I've had no success this year with my roses. Providence has been mighty good to you." ❦ "Providence nothing," said the landowner. "Horse shit."

295

A traveling salesman was planning his first trip to Chicago. The women in that city, a friend told him, are about the wildest in the world. So he was prepared to be accosted. But to his chagrin he only had a dollar with him when it happened. "I'm awful sorry," he told the lady, "but I can't afford to take you to no hotels." ❦ "That's all right," said she. "Come on up to my flat." ❡ "How much will you charge me there?" asked the salesman. "Five dollars," said the lady. ❡ "I would like to very much," said the stranger. "But I only got with me just now one dollar." "Well," said she, "then we'll have to go into an alley. Follow me." ❡ Cohen, by this time thoroughly erect, went after the woman. When they stopped, finally, in the shadow of a dark alley, his penis was like a ramrod. ❡ "Give me your dollar," said the woman. And he did. ❡ "Now let down your pants." Just as he did this she turned and ran away. Pursuit being useless, in his condition, Cohen seized his eager tool, and beginning to rub it up and down, said with a shrug of his shoulders, "*Nu*, so long as I'm here. . . ."

296

A SOUTHERN toast: "Here's high trotting horses, rough roads and porcupine saddles for my enemies!"

297

A CCORDING to a new ruling, whenever there is a circumcision in a Jewish family there must be a policeman present. To keep the piece, of course.

298

A RUSSIAN nobleman, who had become a refugee in Paris, after the successful establishment of the Bolshevik regime, had gained a reputation as one of the most discriminating connoisseurs of feminine wares in that city of connoisseurs. As may well be understood he had not attained this distinction without paying

heavily for it. He was also the most *blasé* man in Paris.
❡ As he strolled down the *Boulevard de la Madeleine*
one Summer's night the approaches of those girls which
tickle more than the vanity of the American visitor were
only insufferable annoyances to him. He was particularly
vexed by one girl who insisted if he come with her she
would offer him a refinement he had never known before and would not ever know again. "Impossible," he
asserted with the finality of the savant, shook her off,
and continued complacently with the delusion that for
him there was nothing new in woman. But in ten minutes the same girl approached him again at another
corner, and again as earnestly renewed the eulogies of
her capacity. "Monsieur, I assure you you will put
it in a place where you have never put it before." Now
this Russian had indeed seriously studied the erotic possibilities of the feminine body. He was willing to wager
any amount of money this *cocotte* could offer him no
sensation with which he was not already familiar to
satiety. So, to get rid of the girl he finally proposed a
bet with her. If she could offer him any orifice, or semb-
lance of orifice, or arrangement of cutaneous surface
which could serve voluptuously to induce the masculine
venereal spasm he would give her a thousand francs.
If not she was to give him a hundred francs of her
earnings through this accomplishment of which she
boasted. ❡ She did not hesitate an instant, and they
were soon in her room. He dropped into a bored attitude on a chair. She held out her mouth sweetly to him.
He shuddered at the thought of the practice which is
by no means unique with man. "No, monsieur, it is not
that," she hastily assured him. She let one sleeve of
her blouse off, disclosing a plump arm-pit. Again he

arched his brows and wearily shook his head. Her
breasts were next bared to his eyes. Close and bounti-
ful as they were, their possibilities offered him nothing
"O, monsieur, you do not think I meant that!" When
she was entirely naked with the exception of her hat and
the veil which came half over her face, he saw only
another specimen, excellent though it was, of the familiar subject of his many minute and painstaking experi-
ments to improve on nature. There was not even any
abnormality visible, no wound that had healed open,
no naturel growth or unnatural excrescence that offered
the possibility of anything new to him. He flicked the
ash from his cigarette and rose to claim his bet. But,
as he raised his eyes he lost for a fraction of a second
his air of utter boredom. She was unscrewing a false
eye. "Put it back," he said with consummate indiffer-
ence, "put it back, and put on your clothes. You win."

299

I N THAT city which, of all American cities, offers most
opportunity for the study of American character,
male and female, we believe must also be placed the
origin of the following tale. ❡ It was at the *Café de la
Paix*. An Englishman had just ordered the *garçon* to
serve him two eggs with his whiskey. An American at
an adjoining table earnestly watched the fellow drop
them into his liquor and swallow the whole at a gulp.
"Pardon me," said the American, "but may I ask you
why you take eggs with your drink." The Englishman
looked at him not without some disdain. "First of all,
because it is none of your business. Second, because I
like it so. And third, because I want to put some lead

in my pencil." The American was a little puzzled. But the attitude of the man did not encourage further questions, so he remained satisfied. ❡ The next time he visited the famous café on the *Place de l'Opéra*, he was determined he would profit by what he had learned of European manners, and ordered his drink according to the best tradition. "*Garçon*," he said to the waiter, "I want two eggs with my whiskey." "Bien, monsieur." But when the order came he could not bring himself to spoil the good whiskey with eggs in it. The waiter approached to serve it for him. "Don't put those eggs in my whiskey," he said. "Mais, pourquoi? Monsieur ask . . ." "Yes. But I don't want them in my whiskey. And if you want to know why, I'll tell you. First, because it's none of your business. Second, because I like it so. And third, because I have no one to write to."

300

WHICH, of course reminds all of us of the rather too experienced chap who married a naive young thing. On climbing naked between the sheets she noticed he carried a huge fountain pen. "But, dear, what have you got your pen for?" "Oh," he explained, to her confusion. "I thought if I couldn't come I'd write."

301

WHICH in turn brings to mind an identical scene, the beginning of married life for a similarly-mated couple. This old roué had been especially anxious to plow a virgin field for once in his life, and had chosen from a convent school. It was chilly, and Marie hurriedly threw off her clothes, climbed under

the covers, and threw her legs in position, one on either
side of the wide bed. The old boy approached her in
the dark, felt for her feet. "Is u little tootsie cold?
Why where is other 'ittle tootsie?" he asked apprehen-
sively.

302

DURING an investigation into swindling by stockbrokers,
the story was told of a woman who entered a broker's
office, with five hundred dollars to invest in a stock. "But"
she said, "I want to be sure I get proper intercourse."
"What's that?" asked the clerk. "I mean," said the woman,
"that I'm a hard-working woman and I want to invest this
five hundred in a good stock, but I want to be sure I get
proper intercourse." "Oh, you mean interest," said the
clerk. "No, I mean intercourse," she insisted. "I've been
fucked before."

303

A YOUNG man was playing with his sweetheart and
tried to slip his hand under her skirts. "Please
don't," she said. "My mother made me promise never
to let a fellow put his hand under my skirts. But if
you'll put your hand down my back, it's the second hole
you come to!"

304

HE SWAGGERED to the bar and called for drinks
for everyone in the room. "What's the idea?
What are you celebrating?" he was asked. ❡ "Come

on, everybody drink," he shouted. "The wife just gave birth to a baby. Roosevelt can be proud of me. I'm a daddy. Some kid, I got." ❡ "What the hell are you bragging about," said one of the gang. "It was a cinch for you. Your wife went through all that pain and suffering. What the hell you got to brag about?" ❡ The new parent straightened up. "Well, I give her the idea, didn't I?"

305

Niagara Falls! The bride's second great dissappointment!

306

A fellow invited a girl friend into one of those F. O. W.* cars, and when they were some way into the country, he asked her to prepare for a screw. She refused. He gave her the alternative, to walk. ❡ "How far are we from town?" asked the girl. ❡ "About seven miles," said the man. ❡ "I'll walk," she said. ❡ Exasperated, he turned round and left her to do so. In a few moments, however, he regretted his cruelty. He waited till she came up to him, took her in again and drove her home. ❡ The following week he again asked her to take a ride. She again accepted. This time he drove very fast and they were soon a long way into the country. Then he again asked her for a piece. Again she refused, and again he told her she could walk. ❡ "How far are we from the city?" she asked. ❡ "Fif-

---

* For the benefit of those not *au courant* with the new additions to the vocabulary of the vernacular we may be pardoned for explaining that F. O. W. is an abbreviation for *fuck or walk*.

teen miles," said he. ⓒ "All right, I give up. You
can have it." ⓒ Overjoyed, her companion screwed
her, with great zest, you may be sure. When he had
finished he could not refrain from asking "Why is it
you were willing to walk seven miles, just as if, let us
say, you were a virgin; but when it came to fifteen you
gave in?" ⓒ "I'm a regular feller," said the girl,
"and I'd walk seven miles any time to save a friend of
mine from a clap, but fifteen miles, never!"

307

A N OLD rake, determined to marry an innocent girl,
went to a convent to select the choice of his heart.
He found there an admirable young woman whom he
readily persuaded to come with him. He took her about
the city, to show her the sights, and immediately after
the marriage ceremony, accompanied him to his hotel.
As they sat in the lobby a number of beautiful women,
unescorted, passed before them. ⓒ "Why are those
women alone?" asked the girl. "And how is it they are
dressed so much better than I am?" ⓒ "Why those are
fast women," said the rake. ⓒ "What's a fast woman?"
asked the girl. ⓒ Pleased, the rake told his young bride
that a fast woman was one who received fifty or a hundred dollars a night for sleeping with a man. ⓒ "They
get all that money?" the girl queried, amazed. "Why,
the priests only gave us an apple."

308

"W HAT's an envelope chemise?" an ignorant youth
asked his flame. ⓒ "Why," said she, "that's
the curtain in front of the smallest theatre in the world.

It plays to an audience of one, and he must remain standing throughout the entire performance."

309

MURPHY came home drunk. His wife was in bed with her lover when she heard him open the door. "Don't move," she said to her paramour. "He's stewed. When he gets into bed he'll fall right asleep. Then you can slip out safely." ❡ Murphy staggered into the room, threw off his clothes and jumped into bed. Suddenly he started. "Wife," he said sternly, "there's someone else in bed with us. I see six feet!" ❡ "Nonsense," said his wife. ❡ "All right, I'll count 'em for ye," said Murphy, crawling out of bed. "One, two, three, four .. Yer right! There's only four." Crawling back into bed, he went peacably to sleep.

310

A FAG was complaining to his friend that when he got home the night before he found a man in bed with his wife. ❡ "What did you do?" his friend asked, all excitement.. ❡ "Do?" said the fairy. "I certainly showed my displeasure The way I slammed the door when I went out she knew I wasn't pleased!"

311

AN OLD sea captain took with him on a long voyage, a whore for his special use. The first morning they were out she stuck her head out of the cabin and called to the commander. "You're going to use me before breakfast, aren't you, Captain," she asked. ❡ The

Captain gazed on her with admiration and, turning
to some passengers nearby, he said soulfully, "Cunt
enough for a thousand men, and it's all mine!"

312

A HENPECKED husband begged off one evening to
go to a stag party. There would be only men
there, he pleaded, so his wife needn't be jealous. But
to his horror, when he arrived he found four naked
women dancing. He called up his wife immediately.
"Unintentionally, dearest, I told you a lie," he said.
"I thought there would be only men here, but now
naked girls are dancing about. What shall I do?"
❡ "If you think you can do anything, come right home,"
said his wife.

313

THE doctor came out of the room in which Perkins'
wife was in child-labor. "It's twins," he announced
to the waiting father. ❡ Perkins face registered perplexity and vexation. "But, doctor," he explained, "I
only stayed with my wife once!"

314

THREE travellers met in the Orient under such aus-
picious circumstances that they decided to continue
their journey together. When they reached Turkey
all evinced a desire to visit a harem. One of the three,
the oldest, approached the eunuch of one of the seraglios and
entered into negotiations with him. The Turk was at first
afraid. "Only eunuchs are allowed in the harem," he said.
"If you get an erection the guards will seize you, and you'll

be killed." "Don't worry," said the man handing the eunuch some money. "Them Turkish whores can't raise a hard on on us." So the trio, stripped to the skin, were led into the Caliph's harem. At the first wiggle by one of the dancing girls, however, the three pricks stood erect and hard. The guards rushed at the intruders, and, seizing them, brought them before the kadi. "Off with their heads," was the order. But when they pleaded that they were foreigners and entitled to some consideration the kadi relented. "What is your occupation?" he asked the first man. "I'm a humble person," said he. "I'm just a woodchopper." "Chop his off," ordered the judge. "And you? What do you do?" he asked. "I'm a blacksmith," said the second. "Put his on the anvil and beat it to a pulp," ordered the kadi. Then, turning to the last, the eldest, he asked him what was his occupation. "I'm a nobody," said the man. "I peddle lollypops."

315

A WOMAN had just been delivered of a child, and the doctor brought out the infant, swathed in a cloth. ❡ "What is it?" asked an inquisitive relative, running her hand up under the cloth. "Ah, a boy." ❡ "Boy nothing," said the doctor. "Let go my finger!"

316

"IT's BEEN a very bad season, hasn't it?" said one actor to another. ❡ "Yep. Outside the *Friars' Club* they're picking up condoms with patches and laundry marks on 'em."

317

A DISTINGUISHED Shakespearean actor and an eminent English critic were at lunch together in a London club, when the conversation, as was natural, turned to the Bard of Avon. ⁅ "Tell me," asked the critic of the actor, "is it your opinion that Shakespeare intended us to understand that Hamlet screwed Ophelia?" ⁅ "I don't know what Shakespeare intended," said the tragedian. "Anyway, I always do."

318

AN AGED man went to a doctor and complained that he could no longer to raise an erection. ⁅ "How old are you?" asked the physician. ⁅ "A hundred and ten," said the man. ⁅ "When did you first notice your incapacity?" he was asked. ⁅ "Just this morning," he replied. ⁅ "Well, I'm afraid there's no hope for you," the doctor replied. "You're much too old for this sort of thing." ⁅ "Well, then, doc," pleaded the old man, "give me something to take the ideas out of my mind."

319

"NO INDEED Mary can't go with ye to the ball," said an Irish mother to her daughter's suitor. Pointing to Mary, whose stomach was quite high, she continued, "Look at Mary from the last two balls!"

320

"YOU'RE asking am I a good cook?" said the wife of a travelling man to a friend. "Why, my Abie is just crazy for the pot roast I make. In fact, when he

comes home from the road that's the second thing he
asks for!"

321

THE following conversation has been reported to us as
occurring between two morons during a lull in the
Sunday morning service. "Who is the venereal old gen'man
maturbatin' up an' down the aisle?" asked one, in low tones.
"You mean the man with the testicle on his eye?" "Yes."
"Why he's the rectum of our constipation." "You don't say!
Why, I never met the old pisspotalien. Take me over and
seduce me."

322

THE minister was reading several announcements
from the pulpit. "The Sisters of Charity will meet
at nine o'clock Tuesday evening. The ladies of the sewing circle are to meet in Mrs. Brown's house Wednesday
evening, and the newly organized Society of Little
Mothers will have its first meeting on Thursday night.
If there are any ladies in the congregation desirous of
becoming Little Mothers will they please speak to the
minister after services."

323

"I LIVE in a real swell neighborhood on the drive,"
said Cohen to his friend. "When I come home at
night, you ought to see the beautiful women. They're
dressed so swell and they look so nice, you would never
take them for whores!"

324

"WHAT are you doing on this train?" one Jew asked another. "I thought you had to stick close to your business in Tulsa." ❡ "Sh, sh," said his friend, "the Klux is after me." ❡ "After a nobody like you? Why?" asked the first. ❡ "A little notting," his friend answered. "I only knocked up the Kleagle's wife and the whole klan is chasing me!"

325

THE original of the above story is said to have been in circulation during the time of the Spanish Inquisition. A Jewish man finding a friend frantically making preparations to flee the city could not imagine why he should be in such a hurry. "I thought nobody knew you for a Jew in Barcelona," he said. "Why, then, are you running away?" "Over a trifle," his friend is said to have replied. "I have caused Torquemada's mistress to be with child and now all the Inquisitors pursue me."

326

"THE truly perfect composition," lectured a Professor of English at Harvard, "embodies an appeal to the imagination, has in it something of religion, and is besides, for these modern times, somewhat *risqué*." ❡ A number of composition were submitted by the class, each striving to exemplify these salient points. The one the professor considered best he read to the class at the following lecture. ❡ It began thus: " 'My God,' said the Duchess, 'take your hand off my . . leg.' "

327

A FAIRY had returned to America from a trip to
England. ⟨ "Oh, I had the loveliest time" he
was telling an acquaintance. "I was entertained by the
best people. You'll never guess whom I was chums
with. Give up? Well, for over two weeks I was with
the Prince of Wales day and night. He became very
fond of me, really." ⟨ "That's all right," said his
friend. "But no matter how much he loves you, you'll
never be Queen."

328

A FRENCH girl who was a guest at a Long Island
home was rapidly learning the English language.
Whenever she came across an unfamiliar word she always asked her hostess what it meant. One day she
startled that lady by asking, in front of her husband,
what the word 'fuck' might mean. ⟨ "Why,-er," said
the lady, greatly embarrassed, "that word means, to -
er, serve. That's it,—to serve." ⟨ At a dinner given
a few days later the French girl haughtily addressed
the butler. "Please to fuck the duck, James." ⟨ "How
jolly!" said one of the guests, an Englishman. "Quaint
conceit, to have the butler fuck the duck. Madam, may
I have the honor to stick my prick in the mashed po-
tatoes?"

329

A STORY told about Ben Peale, the actor, has since been
foisted on many others. He was reproving a certain
chorine for coming late to rehearsals. "But, Ben, . . ." she

began. " 'Ben' in bed," said the actor sternly. "Mr. Peale here!"

330

"I NEVER screw in the morning," said a certain well-known opera tenor. "Not only is it bad for the voice. It's bad for the health generally. Besides, you never can tell whom you're liable to meet during the day!"*

331

A DOCTOR was lecturing to a class of students. "Now take the seminal fluid," he was saying. "One pint of seminal fluid is equal to a pound of blood." One of the students raised his hand and waggled it. "If what you say is so," he asked, "doctor, in case I'm called to a case suddenly, and the man needs bleeding, is it all right to jerk him off?"

332

A MAN entered a bawdy house in a great hurry. "Give me a girl that has a clap," he demanded. ⁌ The madam looked her indignation. Angrily she informed him that such girls were not retained in her establishment. ⁌ "I'll have to go some place else, then," said the man. ⁌ One of the girls, overhearing

---

* It is, of course, well known that, in both man and woman, the pitch of the voice is lower after the orgasm. In spite of the fact that tenors inspire many nice ladies with even more than vicarious sexual satisfaction, they have a reputation of being poor performers on woman. In these implications must lie that which this anecdote contains of humor. Otherwise the reader must grant us indulgence for having included it in this collection. (Editor.)

the conversation, called the madam aside. "Tell him I've got a clap," she said. "Why shouldn't I make the money." ❡ So the madam called the man back, pointed out the girl to him, and they went upstairs. ❡ When he had finished screwing her, the girl looked up at him and simpered, "I fooled you, mister. I ain't got any clap." ❡ "Oh, yes you have," said the man.

333

AN IRISHMAN returned to his home after a day's hard labor, and, removing his shoes, made himself comfortable. His wife came into the room from her washing, fanning her body with her apron. ❡ "Phew, Mike," she said, "but yer feet stink." ❡ "Well, you ought to know them's no geranums you're fanning," he said.

334

THE girl's father came into the parlor and found a young man there. "What are you doing here?" he asked sternly. ❡ "I'm going to marry your daughter," the youth said. ❡ "What! A bum like you? Never!" ❡ The youth seized him by the nose and twisted it. "I will marry your daughter," he said. ❡ The old man sniffed once or twice, then said with determination: "You'll have to. Sit down."

335

"I'D LIKE very much to get in the chorus," a young girl said to the director. ❡ "I'd like to get you in," he replied. "But you're not developed enough." Yielding at last, however, to her tears and pleading, he said, "Go down to the property man and tell him to give you a false bust." ⟨ In a little while she reappeared, with a pair of enormous breasts on. "Good Christ!" the director ejaculated. "That damn fool didn't give you a bust. That's Faltaff's ass you've got on."

336

ONE OF the stipulations of the entrance test for men who desire to join a secret society, is that they strip and crawl on the beach on their hands and knees. If they do not leave five trails they do not get in.

337

A CITY doctor and a country doctor once exchanged offices, the city doctor yearning for a rest, the country doctor seeking further experience. The country doctor's practice was small, although his town was near the site of the summer camp a large department store maintains for its women employees. ⟨ The two doctors met in September and exchanged experiences. "I guess you haven't had much to do in my district," the country doctor said. ⟨ "Indeed I have," said the city doctor. "You'd be surprised how many carrots and cucumbers I've had to extract from the vaginas of those city girls at the camp."

338

THE conductor of a Chicago orchestra was severely 'roasted' by the leading critic of the biggest Chicago daily for including a certain unfamiliar symphony on a program. He was quite angry at the unmerited abuse, and sat down to reply in vein. "As I write this," he began, "I have before me your criticism. Soon I'll have it in back of me . . ."

339

A YOUNG student was undressing in his bedroom, when he discovered, you may imagine with what joy, that a girl just across the alley was also undressing. They reached a state of nudity together, and then she noticed him. He motioned to her to join him, but she shook her head. The young man raised his window a trifle, and she hers. "Come on over," he whispered. ¶ "How?" the girl asked. ¶ "Walk over on this," the youth said, laying his stiff prick on the sill. ¶ "Yes," said the cautious girl, "but how'll I get back?"

340

ONE OF the most popular of the many Lincoln stories is concerned with the visit to the Emancipator of a man named Bates, who brought his family. ¶ "Permit me, Mr. President," he began, "to introduce my wife, Mrs. Bates, and my daughter, Miss Bates. My young son, Master Bates." ¶ Make him stop it," said Lincoln. "It's a bad habit."

341

"I'VE GOT a good joke on you, Mike," said one Irishman to another. "I was goin' by yer house t' other night and you fergot to pull down yer shades. I could see yer shadow from the street, kissin' yer wife and

liftin' up her skirt. I had a good laugh." ⁌ "The
joke's on you, Tim," said the other, "I wasn't home
last night."

342

A MARRIED man who had been "cheating" got in from
his party, late but safe, and was all but undressed
when his wife who had been watching him out of the
corner of her eye, cried out, "Meyer! Where is your
underwear?" ⁌ "Good God!" said Meyer, "I've
been robbed!"

343

A SAILOR reaching port in a condition of insupport-
able lecherousness, made straight for the brothels.
He got hold of a big girl and began operations at once
in his favorite position, the one variously known as
dog-fashion, the cow-couple, all-fours, et cetera. But,
goaded by the accumulated denial of a long voyage, he
rammed so hurriedly at random, that he lodged at
once in the place nature certainly never intended should
be confounded with the other, even though she placed
them dangerously near together. The prostitute, who
had not contracted for this service, objected. " 'S all,
right, girlie, 'sall right. Any port in a storm."

344

A N ABSENT-MINDED toastmaster was about to introduce the next speaker, a Mr. Hotchkiss. He began in these glowing terms: "Ladies and gentlemen,
the next speaker, whom I am about to introduce to you,

is distinguished by nature as well as by his own efforts. His very name is significant. The last syllable of his name causes beautiful women to thrill; it has been the ambition of brave men to place it on the lips of fair women; your very sweetheart desires it . . I take pleasure in introducing Mr. . . Mr. Hitchcock!"

345

MEYER rushed up to Jake in consternation. "I hear you are going to marry Becky Goldberg," he said. "Don't do it. Everybody in Yonkers screwed that girl." ❡ "Well," said his friend, "is Yonkers such a big city?"

346

WHEN a lady says 'No' she means 'Perhaps.' If she says 'Perhaps,' she means 'Yes.' Of course if she says 'Yes,' she's no lady.

347

THE widow Brown was talking to Mrs. Murphy. "I was lookin' at me stomach the other day," she said, "and I was surprised to find how nice and clear my skin is there. There's hardly a wrinkle, in fact, outside the one I was born with." ❡ Murphy happened to overhear the conversation. "My stomach is as clear as yourn," he interposed, "and as fer wrinkles, mine ain't got any." ❡ "Well my stomach is nicer," snapped the widow. ❡ "Oh, and sure, is it?" said Murphy disdainfully. "I'll put mine agin it any day!" ❡ *Please omit flowers.*

348

A MAN about-town who was also something of a sportsman was one day preparing to go golfing, when his stenograhper came into his office and saw two golf balls on his desk. ❡ "What are those?" she asked. ❡ "Those are golf balls," said her employer. ❡ When she next entered his sanctum she noticed there were four golf balls on the desk. "I see you shot another golf," was her brilliant comment.

349

A WHORE, travelling for her health, stopped at a little town in the West. Her calling soon became known, and she was receiving visits of the men of the town, young and old, married and single. So keen was the ardor of her admirers that they visited her again and again. In fact she had completely demoralized the town. ❡ Finally the elders of the church met and determined to put a stop to the young woman's operations by forcing her out of town. The chief of police was on his vacation, the mayor would not act in the matter, and so it devolved on the elders. A committee of three called on the girl. ❡ "We must approach her gently," said the deacon, "and persuade her to leave without a scandal." But when they got to her house he again said, "Let us not alarm her by a show of force. You gentlemen wait down here and I'll go up and speak to her." . . Which was done. But the moments turned into minutes, and then an hour, and still the deacon had not come down. The two who waited for him began to grumble. One was a butcher, the other a clothing merchant, and they both had business to attend to, without waiting for the deacon. They discussed it between them and the butcher left, the other deciding to wait. ❡ After another half-hour down came the deacon. ❡ "There is nothing for us to do here," he said, shaking his head, "this young woman has been grossly maligned. In the short talk I had with her I found her to be, not a bawd, but a most cultured girl. We have no right to force her to leave town." ❡ "All right," said the other wearily, "if that is your opinion, button your pants and let's go!"

350

Two girls were walking down Fifth Avenue when they passed a certain popular actor. "Hasn't he a handsome profile," exclaimed one of the girls. ❡ "You mean half way down?" said her more experienced friend. "That's no profile, Lil. Believe me, those are keys."

351

Prix: What is it that walks on two legs and has its tail in the ground? Bollix: I give up. ❡ Prix: A widower.

352

"Mother," complained a young bride, "all these three days Harry has made no approach to me. I'm like the day I was married. What shall I do?" ❡ "I never heard of such a bashful man," said her mother. "When you get to bed tonight take his hand and put it on your affair. Then he'll take the hint." ❡ When her daughter came down next morning mother cheerfully asked how the ruse had worked. ❡ I t didn't work at all." ❡ "Didn't you do what I said?" ❡ "Yes, I did as you said. I put his hand on my pussy, and he got up and washed himself!"

353

A MAN who visited a whorehouse was complaining to the madam: "I've had every kind of treatment here. I've been screwed, sucked, jerked, everything. I've tried every way. Haven't you got a new thrill for me?" The madam thought hard for a while, then said, "Have you tried our radio girl?" ❡ "No, what's that? Who's that?" the man asked in surprise. ❡ "Why, it's that girl over there," the madam pointed. "You take her tits, put one in each ear, and hear her coming."

354

THE captain of a small sailing ship used to buy all his supplies at one shop. One day, while he was stocking up for a voyage the owner of this little shop said to him: "Captain, I have here something that will delight you. It is a rubber woman. When you get a week or two out at sea and feel the need of a little recreation blow up this woman. You'll find she's so like the real thing you won't be able to tell the difference." ❡ The captain thanked him and included the package in his personal order. When he was at sea about ten days he thought, with some skepticism, that he would try out the rubber woman. With a little effort he blew her up, and there lay a beautifully formed nude. Just then there was a call for the captain to take the bridge. He rushed from his cabin, first throwing

a sheet over the effigy. In came the first mate, looking
for the captain. He spied what he thought was a woman,
under the sheet. Without hesitation he unbreeched
himself, and set to work. When the ship's commander
returned to his long-waited pleasure, the mate was gone,
and everything was in its proper place. ❡ The voyage
over the captain again went to the little shop for supplies. ❡ "How was that woman? Was she realistic?"
❡ "I'll say she was," answered the captain; "so realistic
she gave me a clap."

355

AN ENGLISHMAN who got mixed up in a poker game
with some friends from America won a big pot.
The man next to him congratulated him. "Lucky dog,"
said he. ❡ "My word!" said the limey. "Are you in-
sulting me." ❡ "Why no," exclaimed his friend.
"That's a term of admiration with us, and quite the
proper thing to say on an occasion like this." ❡ Some
days later the Englishman was playing bridge with his
host and hostess and another guest at a house-party.
His hostess made a grand slam and raked in the stakes.
Admiringly the Englishman leaned over toward her
and said, "Lucky bitch."

356

RONALD came home rather early and found his Mamie
quite flustered. His perturbation was not decreased by
the sight of a wet towel in the bathroom. Ronald quietly
drew out his razor and began to strop it. "What is that wet
towel doing here?" he demanded. "I was feeling miserable,"
said Mamie, "and I wet it and put it on my head, but it ain't

done much good." Ronald kept on stropping. "How come
that bed is all mussed up?" he queried. "I felt so bad, I laid
down, but that ain't done much good either," his wife answered. Ronald began to strop with increasing vigor.
"What are you going to do with that razor?" she asked.
"I'm gonna shave," said Ronald, "if that towel dries out
soft."

357

"IT's GETTING so, nowadays, with fairies and what not
in the public eye," says a famous cartoonist, "that
a couple of fellows can't go anywhere for a week-end
without taking a girl along!"

358

THE story is told of a certain stage star that she
visited a physician for a periodic health examination. ❡ "Please remove your blouse," the doctor asked.
❡ "Oh, my no," objected the actress, who, by the way,
is rather flat chested. "Come, come," said the doctor,
"don't make mountains out of molehills."

359

A WEST Side bruiser, who had seen a bit of life, was
bragging of his adventures to a friend, saying that he had experienced nearly all that life might
offer. ❡ "Have you ever been sucked off?" his friend
asked. ❡ The gorilla looked his surprise. "What is
that?" he asked. ❡ "Oho, you must try it then,"
said his friend, and took him to a house, where he could

have that thrill furnished to him. ⟪ The whore bade him strip, then took his cock in her hand and stroked it delicately. With a silver shaker she sprinkled sugar on it. Then she took some whipped cream and laid that on too. ⟪ "Hold on," said the tough egg, as she was about to seize it between her lips. "I'll take that me-self."

360

A SAILOR who had dropped into one of those Broad-way dance palaces was quite struck by one of the hostesses, and gave her a great deal of attention. As they were dancing their last dance she snuggled up to him and said, "Aren't you going to take me home?" ⟪ "Is there anything in it," asked the tar, brusquely. ⟪ "Just a little dust from dancing," she answered coyly.

361

COHEN and Murphy had been partners for twenty years when suddenly Cohen got it into his head that he wanted to be in business by himself. ⟪ "I don't know, Murph," he said. "I ain't got nottin' against you, but I'd like to try for myself. So I made up my mind we should split." ⟪ Murphy accepted his decision gracefully. ⟪ "Of course," he said, "we'll part friends." ⟪ "Positively, the best," said Cohen. "And now lets call in Feldman, our lawyer, and have him draw up the dissolution papers." ⟪ Feldman, when he heard the news, was grief-stricken. "After twenty years," he moaned. "Of course, I'm getting paid for doing this, but nothing hurts me so much as to have to draw up these papers breaking up this fine partnership. But, Cohen, since you made up your mind, as the Latin phrase has it, *yens de goy*." *

362

A RICH man fleeing from a terrible coup d'etat was at the border of the country with his daughter. Of all his possessions he was able to save only some of his finest jewels which he had given her to hide in her person. They passed the customs safely, and were again seated in the car when the man, whose mind was burdened by the memory of all the rubies, sapphires and diamonds he had had to leave behind, could not refrain from moaning, "Aacht, aacht, Katia, if your mommy wuz only livin'! She could 'av hid 'em all."

363

O BSERVING a female bending over a tub of wash a soldier approached her, and, with a practiced flip of the hand, raised her dresses from behind. He was just about to backscuttle her when, without looking up from her wash, the woman asked, "Officer or private?" "Private," the soldier answered. "Upper hole, upper hole," said the woman.

364

H ENRY lived in the suburbs, and every night travelled home by motor. One night his car stalled a little way from town. When midnight came and he

---

* This, every New Yorker should know, is only a phonetic spelling in Latin characters of a rather frequently employed Yiddish phrase which, literally translated into English, means "screw the Gentile."

had not yet put in an appearance, his wife, worried, sent six telegrams to his closest friends, asking whether they had seen Henry. ⟪ Next morning she received six answers, all reading: "Henry is spending the night with me."

365

IN THE third act of a melodrama that had met thus far with nothing but derision from its audience, a troupe of cavalry was supposed to gallop across the stage in pursuit of the villain. As the horses came on one of them dropped a load of turd. ⟪ "A bit of a critic, eh," observed a man in an aisle seat.

366

A LOCAL shoe dealer has the following sign in his window:

FRENCH HEELS
GOOD FOR STREET WALKING

367

"CAN you come out with the boys tonight?" ⟪ "No, my sister is getting married tonight and I got to stay home and mind her baby."

368

TWO Scots were playing a round of golf one Sunday morning. At the second hole Sandy complained, "Mac, I dinna feel weel. Let's go back to the club hoose." ⟪ His friend told him to brace up. The air would do him good. At the fifth hole Sandy

again complained, "Mac, me stumick is gang aglee."
❡ "Mon, that can happen to all of us," his friend replied. "Take a nip of this and ye'll be richt." ❡ "But
I dinna feel richt, I'm tellin' ye. At the foorth hole I
left a poop." ❡ "That can happen to all of us," his
friend again said. ❡ "I ken, I ken, but I followed
through," said Sandy.

369

Two old Johnnies were discussing a proposed trip
abroad. "We mustn't overlook Paris," said one.
"They. tell me that the preponderance of women over
men is now so great in Paris that swell women pay as
high as twenty-five dollars in American money to be
screwed." ❡ "What of it?" said the other. "You can't
live in Paris on twenty-five dollars a month."

370

A BARKER with a one ring circus that toured the
South used to describe the laughing hyena somewhat as follows: ❡ "We also have inside the big tent
the laughing hyena, most jovial of all the animals.
The laughing hyena eats only once a month. Just once
a month, ladies and gentlemen. He moves his bowels
only once every six months. And he mounts his mate
only once a year. Think of it, ladies and gentlemen.
This animal has intercourse only once every twelve
months. They call him the laughing hyena. Now
ladies and gentlemen, I have a little proposition to offer you. There's a reserved seat in there for any man
or woman who can tell me what the hell he has to
laugh about."

371

J IMMY, fifteen years old, was still in the lower grades, largely because of his proclivities for gambling. He was always ready to bet on anything and everything. What is more, he always won. His father one day complained to his teacher, saying if she could once cause him to lose a bet, he believed the boy would give up the habit. Teacher, quite a comely lady, said she would try. Next morning when she came into the class no one was there but Jimmy. He sniffed as teacher came into the room. "What are you sniffing about?" she asked. ⁋ "Why you smell like you're not well," Jimmy answered. ⁋ That was where teacher knew she had him. ⁋ "I'll bet fifty cents I'm not," she retorted. ⁋ The boy accepted the bet, and, to convince him that she was not ill teacher raised her skirts and let him see her immaculate condition. ⁋ Apparently disgruntled, the boy paid the bet. ⁋ Teacher made it a point to see Jimmy's father that very afternoon. "I believe we've cured him," she said. "He made a bet with me this morning, and lost." ⁋ "What was the bet?" asked the father. ⁋ "Why, he bet fifty cents that I was unwell. To prove I wasn't I raised my skirts and showed him." ⁋ "Gee, whiz," said the parent, "you didn't cure him. Only this morning he bet me five dollars he'd see your privates before tonight."

372

H IRAM had just come back from a six-months visit to the city where he prided himself he had learned a thing or two. The first Saturday night he took his girl out buggy riding. When they were some

way out of town, the yokel astonished the girl by rein-
ing in hard. He threw one arm around her and began
to feel her breasts and run his hand along her thighs.
Suddenly he unbuttoned his trousers and drew out a
stiff pecker. ❡ "Shall I lift my dress?" asked the girl
timidly. ❡ "No," said Hiram, "take that gum out of
your mouth."

373

"C'MAWM, Sarah," pleaded the young boy with the
cook, "gimme a piece, c'mawn, lemme screw ya."
"Go away, child," laughed the woman, "you're too young.
Go along with you." "Aw, c'mon, just a little screw," the
boy pleaded. "Go on away, child, you're too small, I tell
you." But the boy pleaded and pleaded, till finally Sarah
raised her skirts, and standing against the wall, let the boy
put in his penis. The youth was diddling away with the
ardor of puberty, when the girl suddenly said: "C'mon in
bed, child, you've got talent."

374

Two friends, one of them the owner of a car, used
to go 'chippy-cruising' every night. Invariably they
picked up a couple of girls who didn't care in whose
car they rode. One of the friends would mince no
words. "C'mon, pick up your dress and we'll screw,"
was the sum and substance of his conversation. ❡ One
day his friend could endure such grossness no longer.
❡ "Why are you always talking of nothing but screwing?" he remonstrated. "Girls don't like that. Make
conversation, man. Tell them how beautiful they look.

Talk about their clothes, about shows, books, and the like. Don't always talk cunt." ❡ "All right," said the first, "I'll try out your system tonight, for a change." ❡ That evening they again picked up two girls and the following dialogue took place between the direct chap and his girl. ❡ "Have you seen the Chauve Souris?" he asked sweetly. ❡ "No," said the girl. ❡ "Neither have I," said the fellow. "Let's fuck!"

375

WHEN the gold miners came to 'Frisco for their annual jamboree in the gold rush days they used to have the badger game worked on them a little too frequently to please some. One day a hoary miner came to a dance hall in the earthquake city and after doing a turn or two about the floor with an attractive damsel went with her to a booth in the back of the hall where he found a stool. Letting down his trousers he caused the girl to straddle him and was enjoying a luxurious fuck when a hand suddenly reached in and yanked the young woman off him, while a voice shouted, "My wife! My wife!" ❡ Instantly the miner drew two guns and pointed them at the intruder. ❡ "Put that cunt back," he bellowed.

376

WHEN the married man found out the girl was a virgin he declined to have anything to do with her. Let someone else make the road, he said. ❡ "You're smart," sneered the girl; "you want some one else to do the dirty work, and then you'll take all the pleasure." "Sure," he said, "I didn't build the subway, but I ride in it."

377

A YOUNG man was calling on a swell girl, who had a pet Pomeranian. The dog cuddled up on the sofa near them. Suddenly the man, seized by a cramp, passed wind. Embarrassed, he turned to the dog and cuffed him. The incident passed, but again the young man broke wind. Again he cuffed the dog, greatly embarrassed before the swell young girl. But when the dog got up to change his position, the young woman said, "Throw him off the couch, I think he's gonna shit."

378

Z AVIER took his sweetie to the ball game. Marcy didn't know a thing about baseball. But the fella was enlightening her ignorance by his comment on every play. The pitcher curved over a beauty and Zavier said, "Some pitcher." When the batter sent the ball over the fence he exclaimed, "Some batter!" Again the pitcher wound up. "Ball one," bawled the umpire. "Ball one," echoed Zavier. "Ball two," bawled the umpire. "Two balls on him," explained the fella. "Ball three," bawled the umpire. "See that batter, honey?" questioned Zavier. "He's got three balls on him." *Some* man, I'll tell the world," said she.

379

A TRAVELLING man was riding through the country when his car broke down near a farm house. The farmer saw his predicament, and, as it was just past noon, invited him to dinner. He accepted. ❡ At the table one of the children broke wind. "Do you allow the children to fart before you?" asked the traveller, with a frown. ⁋ "We haf no rules aboud it," the farmer answered. "Sometimes they fart first, sometimes I do."

380

I T WAS in a western restaurant, and a tall and a short man stood at the counter when a woman came in and stood near them. Suddenly the short man let one go. "Madam," said the tall man, "did you hear that little son-of-a-bitch fart?" ⁋ The lady drew herself up haughtily. "I didn't come in here to be insulted," she said. ⁋ "Neither did I, madam," said the tall man. "If the little bastard does it again, I'll kick him in the ass."

381

"W HAT'S that, mam'selle?" the little boy questioned his governess, as he pointed at the penis of the elephant. The zoo's elephant was busy pissing. ⁋ "You mean ze trunk?" asked the lady. ⁋ "No," said the boy, "that thing hanging down in the middle." ⁋ "Oh, you mean ze tail," the lady said. ⁋ "No, no, that thing there," the child insisted, pointing straight at it. ⁋ "Oh, zat, zat is nothing," said the governess. ⁋ A Frenchman who was standing nearby tipped his hat. "Mam'selle is blasé", he said, lifting his eyebrows.

382

"I THINK I'm married to a rabbit," complained a woman in North Dakota to her lawyer. "He no sooner mounts me than he shoots his load and is through.

I can get no satisfaction out of him, and I want a divorce." ❡ Before the lawyer took the case he desired to look up the law on the subject, so he asked the woman to return next day and he would advise her. ❡ When she came in he said to her: "Madame, I have carefully looked up the law in your case, and I'm sorry to say there's nothing you can do about it. In this state, when the man is through, the woman is fucked."

383

WILLIE caught a squirrel and brought it to school. But the nervous little beast escaped him, and ran frantically about the room looking for a place of escape. It found nothing better than the dark recesses under the skirt of the teacher. "Willie, Willie," she shrieked in terror, "get it out, get it out!" "Oh, don't worry, teacher. When he finds there's no nuts up there, he'll come out all right."

384

A ROMANTICALLY inclined sailor was leaving a hard-bellied whore he had fallen in with 'down the line' in San Francisco. "If any thing happens to you in nine months," he said to her in leaving, "you'll call it Fatima, won't you. I like that name." She: "And if anything happens to you in three weeks you can call it eczema if you like that better."

385

IT IS related, in various forms, and always as a true story, that one of the latest of a series of wives, asked to make a few remarks at a dinner, after some

fifteen other speakers had said their say, simply rose and
softly said: "It's been mighty hard for the others, but
it's pretty soft for me." All versions, however, have it
that thereafter she sat down to a gale of merriment.

386

A N AMERICAN in Berlin for the first time, struck by
the cheap prices, treated himself to many luxuries.
Among these was a manicure. Always afraid to try
them in his home town, here he boldly sat in front of
the *fraulein* in the Adlon and let her do his nails. He
soon came to the point where he invited the girl to
dinner and the theatre. She accepted with alacrity.
After the show they went to a cabaret, and then to his
room where that happened which usually happens in
such circumstances. ❡ Some two days later, as he was
strolling down the Friederichsstrasse, he met the mani-
cure-girl again. She saw at once that he was not nearly
as cordial as he had been. "What is it?" she asked.
"Are you angry with me?" ❡ "Why shouldn't I be?"
demanded the American. "Not that I mind so much
that you gave me crabs the other night. But why did you
have to cut my nails so short?"

387

A TRAVELLING man whose territory was within fifty
miles of home was unlucky in his home visits.
Every time he was able to spend a little time with
his wife she was ill, and they both were dissappointed.
At last they agreed she should wire him when things
were all right, and he would run in for the night certain
the flag would be up. ❡ His next trip began one noon.

He had been out only two hours when he received
the following telegram: "See you when tea is ready.
Mary."*

388

A N AMERICAN was being led through an old English
castle by a lackey who was commenting on ob-
jects of interest. They came to the ancestral gallery,
and the servant pointed with pride to one portrait.
⟨ "Sir 'Enry," he said, "distinguished 'imself at the
battle of 'Astings. Lord Robert," pointing to another,
" 'ero of the War of the Roses." And so on, down the
line, extolling each one for one virtue or another. At
last he came to the portrait of an imposing, bewigged,
old gentleman. "Sir William," he said in an awestruck
whisper. ⟨ "What did he do?" asked the American.
⟨ " 'E's the founder of the family." ⟨ "I know, but
what did he do?" ⟨ " 'E's the founder of the family." ⟨ "You've said that before. But what did he
do? What is he distinguished for?" ⟨ 'E's the founder
of the family." ⟨ "Now I understand that perfectly.
But can't you tell me what he did in the daytime?"

389

A NOTED worker for birth-control was lecturing on
the East Side to an audience composed of mostly
Jewish women. She had just told them they should use
a douche after every act of sexual intercourse. ⟨ "Yeh,
yeh," said one of the wives, "go be an acrobat. Six times
a night I should run to de sink yet."

* We believe there is an error in the transcription of this tale; that "tea" should be
"T," T for Thomas, a name sometimes given to the active male organ of generation.
Yet, even granting this to be the case, the humor here is not irresistible. (Editor.)

390

A soldier and his lady friend were in the latter's parlor. "Honey," said he, "I'm leavin' for France in the morning. Won't you be good to me tonight, and let me screw you?" ❡ "What?" shrilled the girl, "how dare you. The idea of saying such a thing to me. Go away. Leave me at once. The idea." ❡ "All right," said the soldier, "leggo my cock and I'll go."

391

"I feel great," said one man to another. ❡ "Why you look lousy," the other objected. ❡ "I know I look lousy, but I feel great," said the first. ❡ "All right, Mr. Cunt," said the other. ❡ "Come on, now! What d'ya mean calling me a name like that?" demanded the first. ❡ "Well, that's the only thing I know that looks so lousy and feels so good."

392

A certain editor published a tirade against lewdness with which he said the New York theatre was infested. Among other occupations was one that leading men make violent, physical love to minor actresses in their dressing rooms and that leading actresses seduce the younger actors. ❡ Soon after the article was published the editor was openly accused at the *Friar's Club* of having peeped through the keyholes of dressing rooms to get his material. ❡ "How could I?" was his defense. "The keyholes were stuffed."

393

Mrs. Malone and her husband were always quarreling. It got on the nerves not only of themselves, but of the neighbors. One of these finally expostulated with Mrs. Malone. "Trate the man nice," she said. "Whin he comes home bring him his slippers, light his pipe fer him, wear a niglijay and sit on his lap. Make the ould man comfy." Mrs. Maloney determined to try it. ❡ So that evening when Pat came home he was greeted like a lover by his mistress. Mrs. Malone had turned the light low, and was in a transparent flimsy. She threw her arms about his neck and kissed him lusciously. Leading him to a soft chair she brought his slippers, filled his pipe and lit it for him. Then she cuddled up on his lap and began to fondle him. "Let's go to bed, dearie?" she whispered sweetly. ❡ "We might as well," said Pat. "I'll get hell when I get home anyway."

394

An itinerant Italian musician, one of those with a dancing bear, rode in a Pullman from St. Louis to Denver. His bear he tied up in the baggage car. That evening, when the berths had been made up, the Italian went to the front of the train to see that his bear had received his food and water. He discovered the animal had disappeared. Frantic, he started on a hunt through the cars for his pet. It was nowhere to be seen. He was about to give up and resign himself to the regret that the beast had broken loose and, seeking freedom, had leaped out of the car, when his attention was arrested by a voice in a lower berth ❡ "I won't." It was the voice of a woman in passion. "Stop hugging me." The Italian rested easily, but waited discreetly "Well, you might at least be a geneltman and take off your fur coat." ❡ In due time the bear was docile again.—*With apologies to old maids.*

395

"WHY are your thighs so scratched?" asked a young man of a woman he was about to screw. ❡ "Well, you see," said she, "my husband's a Mexican and wears ear rings."

396

A TRAVELLING man who was making Carnegie, Pensylvania, was struck by a beautiful blonde waitress, with whom he made a date. That night they stepped out, and wound up in his room at the hotel. When the girl had stripped, the drummer noticed an anomaly which caused him to exclaim in surprise, "Why, how's this? Your hair's all black down here, while your head's as blond as they make 'em." ❡ "Yesterday was payday at the mines," said the girl.

397

COHEN and Teplitzky went into partnership, manufacturing condoms. "You know, Tep," said Cohen, "if we could only advertise this article, we could clean up a fortune." ❡ "*Nu*, but how can we do that?" ❡ "Let's go to an advertising agency," suggested the enterprising Cohen. ❡ So they called on a number of agencies, but were indignantly shown the

door at each. Back in the office, Cohen was undaunted.
"Smart people, these agencies. Come in early tomorrow,
Tep, old man, and I'll show you an ad that I'll write
myself that all the newspapers and magazines can
print." ❡ "Yeh, yeh," said he of the old school. "The
smartest advertising brains in America can't do it, and
you'll write me such an ad." ❡ But next morning,
there was the ad:

IF YOU WANT CHILDREN
THAT'S YOUR BUSINESS

IF YOU DON'T
THAT'S OURS

398

A CHAP who had his girl out for a ride in his Ford
stopped for a moment to get a package of cigar-
rettes, but left the engine running. The gentle vibration
of the machine set up a sympathetic trembling in the
young woman. When her beau came out she called to
him passionately, "K-k-iss m-m-e! Charlie, I'm coming."

399

A TENNESEE engineer with a pretty daughter had an
assistant who showed extraordinary qualities as
a machinist and was quiet and well-behaved besides.
The father introduced his helper to his daughter and
the match was soon arranged. After the marriage, however, the son-in-law drew away and the father-in-law
tired his wits trying to guess the reason of the estrange-
ment. At length he boldly asked his son-in-law the reason for his sudden coldness. "You know I mean right,

Bill," he began earnestly and if I've made a mistake I'll do all I kin to make up for it. Waren't the goods according to specification? Waren't she a virgin?" ⟨ "It don't matter nothin'," replied Bill, still disgruntled. ⟨ "Treat me fair, Bill," cried the father. "Tell me, war she a virgin or warn't she?" ⟨ "How can I tell," exclaimed Bill. "All I can say is, I never knowed a virgin before that had that cinder-shifting movement."

400

"I SAY, Mary, would you just as soon—?" "Look here, Jim Jackson, don't get fresh with me! My name's Miss Smith, not Mary. I only allow my best and most intimate friends to call me Mary." "I beg your pardon, Miss Smith. But say, Miss Smith, would you mind moving your ass a little to the left. One of my balls is caught."

401

MARY had lived with Jack for many months, and there was nothing she hadn't done for him, from sucking his balls to his arse. She had stopped at no licentiousness. He had screwed her and back-scuttled her. After a time, however, they had a falling out, and parted as casually as they had come together. ⟨ Four or five months later he saw her on Broadway. He had always kept a tender place for her in his memory, he had good reason to. So he went up to her, and greeted her warmly. Something of the old flame, again surged up in him, and he asked her to come again to his apartment. ⟨ "No," said Mary, "I can't. I'm married now. And I wan t you to understand I told my husband everything." ❡ "You told him everything? All about the little parties we used to have, you know?" leered Jack. ❡ "Yes," said Mary. "Everything." ❡ "Well, I don't know which to admire most, your gall or your memory," said he.

402

BEFORE the races Alexander took his girl around to the stables to look over the horses to see if they couldn't pick a winner. The first stall they looked into was that of a young stallion with a good record. The beast was in fine fettle, evidently, the way he was waving the distinguished mark of his horsehood. Pearl considered it a while with sufficient interest. Then drawing her man away, she said, "Don't bet on him, Alec. That horse isn't gonna win. He hasn't got his mind on his business."

403

WALTERS was very fond of his daughter, who was very pretty and just turning five years old, so, while his wife was away, he gave a bachelor party to some of his cronies, in order that they might see how smart his young offspring was. ❡ It must be admitted, however, that most of his cronies came, not to see the daughter, but the pretty governess. ❡ They wondered why the Missus had left the slow, old Walters alone with the governess, who was quite "easy" to look upon. ❡ If their *curiosity* had been great, their *envy* was greater when they gave the governess the once over. She was a 'pip.' ❡ When she came in with the child it ran to one of the guests and started prattling. "Me slept with Daddy last night," she said. ⁋ That's not right," said the governess. "You mean, '*I* slept with Daddy.' " Then a faint dash of color came to her cheeks, and the cronies wondered, as they went home, whether Walters was really as slow as they took him to be.

404

A VERY filthy, but withal humorous, story is told of the Captain who made it a strict rule aboard his ship that buggery was not to be tolerated. Other forms of relieving one's passions were, however, not excluded. Imagine, then, his anger when one of the crew, respectfully saluting him, said: "Captain, there's been buggery aboard ship." ⁋ "What!" roared the skipper. ⁋ "There's been buggery aboard ship," said the sailor, firmly. "I tasted shit on the first mate's balls."

405

G US had opened a new saloon in those pre-poisonous days. When he had been operating a week his friend Krause came in. "Vell, Gus, you pin goin' a veek now. How iss business?" ⁋ "Lousy, Adolf" said Gus, "All I pin doin' is tradin' ice-watre for piss all week long."

406

A N OLD tailor riding on a train to Albany was eyeing too men on the seat opposite him. One of these men had on handcuffs, an article of wearing apparel utterly unfamiliar to the tailor. Unable any longer to restrain his curiosity he ventured timidly to ask the guard what was the matter with his companion that he had to wear a thing like that. "Bugs," said the keeper briefly. "What?" asked the tailor. "Nuts," said the other. The man raised his hands in horror. "He's got bugs on his nuts and you keep his hands tied up like that?"

407

AN ENGLISHMAN and an American were the sole occupants of the same compartment on a continental train. "There seem to be no lavatory accommodations on this train," said the Englishman, "and I have a severe cramp. So would you mind if I relieved myself here?" ❡ The American nodded that it was all right with him, and the Englishman carefully spread out a copy of the *London Times*, on which he crapped with precision. When he was through he folded the paper and dropped it out of the window. ❡ In the meantime the American had drawn a long, black cigar from his vest pocket and proceeded to light up. "I say, you know," the Englishman protested, "this is no smoking compartment."

408

THE witness in a rape case was giving his testimony: "I seen the man lay down the girl, Judge," he said. "Then he took out his prick . . ." ❡ "Hold on," interrupted the Judge. "You can't use such a word in a Court of Justice. Say 'penis.'" ❡ "Well, he took out his penis," continued the witness, "and stuck it into her cunt . . ." ❡ "Hold on," said the Judge, "are you so ignorant you don't know the proper words for these

parts of the body. Say 'vagina.'" ¶ "But, Judge, it
was her cunt." ¶ "Do as I say, or I'll hold you in con-
tempt," thundered his Honor. ¶ "What' that?"
asked the witness. ¶ "That's a technicality of the law
about which you evidently know nothing." ¶"All
right, Judge, in her vagina. And then he give her the
Chicago stroke." ¶ "The 'Chicago stroke?' What's
that?" asked the magistrate. ¶ "That's a technicality
of fucking, Judge, about which *you* evidently know
nothing."

409

THE patient reader should by now have been suffi-
ciently annoyed by endeavors to resolve the riddle of Solomon which was proposed on page 11. For
this could not possibly be expounded by one of ordinary human wisdom, and other than such cannot be
expected to read here. But to the shining intelligence
of Ris 'tis easy. "He made them all lie naked flat on
their backs on the floor. Then he went around with a
little pot of water and poured a few drops in the navel
of each. Those that sizzled he screwed."

410

THERE IS in the conundrum line one which can be
asked in any company with absolute certainty of
being secure from reproach. ¶ "What is it a hound
does on three legs, a man standing up, and a woman sitting down?" ¶"Shakes hands, of course!"

411

A YOUNG chambermaid accused a bellboy in the hotel
of raping her. She was giving her testimony in court:

"You see, Judge, I was cleaning out one of the rooms, when I heard a band playing and I looked out the window. There was the Mayor coming down the street, with flags flying and two bands making music. But suddenly, this here youth comes up behind me, shuts down the window on me, and rapes me from behind." "Didn't you struggle?" asked the defendant's counsel. "I sure did," said the girl, "but he had the window down on me." "Well, why didn't you yell?" asked the State's attorney. "I didn't want people to think I was cheering a Democratic Mayor," she answered simply.

412

NAT, a comic, was recounting an adventure he had in Paris. "An Apache ran up to me," he said, "held a gun against my breast, and said: 'Go down on me, or I shoot.'" "Well, what did you do?" asked one of his auditors. "I'm here, ain't I?" said Nat.

413

"I HAD a funny dream last night," said a woman to her husband. "I dreamt that I was in a huge auction room and they were auctioning off cocks. John Barrymore's brought five thousand dollars. Lou Tellegen's brought the same. Lowell Sherman's brought two thousand and so on, down the line." ¶ "Is that so?" her husband asked, "what did cocks like mine bring?" ¶ "Oh, they were sold in lots, at a dollar the lot." ¶ "Well, I had a dream last night, too," said the man. "But I dreamed of cunts. They were auctioning them off, in a huge place, too, and Cleopatra's brought fifteen thousand dollars. That of Helen of Troy went for thirteen thousand. That of Follies' girls brought a thousand apiece and so on, down the line." ❡ "What did cunts like mine bring?" the wife demanded. ❡ "Oh," said her husband, "that's where they held the auction."

414

A YOUNG man who was visiting a whorehouse about three o'clock one morning was greatly surprised to find his father there. "Well," said he, severely, "to find my own father in a place like this. Have you no respect for me? None for your marriage vows?" ❡ "Don't be angry, sonny," said the old man. "You wouldn't have me wake up mamma this hour of the night for a dollar, would you?"

415

A MAN accused of rape interposed this novel defense: "Your Honor," he said, "I wasn't within a mile of the place where this woman says she was raped. Besides, I didn't rape her, she asked me to fuck her. And, anyway, that ain't the woman I fucked!"

416

A CITY man who had bought a farm took his cow one day to a neighboring farmer whose bull was at stud. As the bull was ramming his animal he noticed the farmer's daughter, a buxom lass of nineteen, watching the operation. "Some bull," he ventured. The girl nodded. ❡ "Does his work well, doesn't he?" he said

leering. Then, as he stepped closer to her, he whispered,
"Believe me, I'd like to do what that bull is doing."
❡ "Why don't you?" said the girl pertly. "It's your
cow."

417

O PPOSITE the aisle from a young couple on their way
to the Falls for their honeymoon sat a stranger,
whom the benedict engaged in conversation while the
bride was washing. Finally, the porter having meanwhile made up the bridal berth, the young man
stretched, and said: "Well, guess I'll have to start the
old steam engine going." ❡ The other rose and
stretched, too. "Guess I'll get the hand car ready,"
said he.

418

A N OLD fellow, who was the father of nineteen children, and who had been severely admonished by his
social worker not to have another, had to confess that number twenty was on the way. "You'll have to give up intercourse," he was told. "I sure would like to," said the fellow.
"But that old pecker of mine is powerful insistent." "Well,
we can easily fix that," said his worker. "The county
doesn't want any more of your offspring on the public
charge, so we'll just cut off your pecker." The man did not
protest, and it was done. Still, the following year, he again
had to report that he was about to become a father. "The
fault ain't mine this time, boss," he said "as well you know.
It's all the fault of that old woman of mine who's got a cunt
that would suck up a tack."

419

"HAVE you noticed the indecent billboards around New York?" asked an English visitor. "I refer particularly to an advertisement issued by a soap organization. It reads: 'Women love to wash their fine things in Lux.'"

420

AN EIGHTEEN-YEAR-OLD child of the city, a freshman at an Eastern University, was out on a hiking trip with a "pal," a youth from Massachusetts. One evening toward dusk rain came up and they sought accommodations in a farm house. "But, Bill," the good wife said to her mate, "we only got that foldin' bed in the back parlor." "Oh, that'll be fine," the girl promptly said. "You know we've only been married a week." When the two children were alone together preparing for the night the boy, to re-assure her of his irreproachable probity said, "I'll put the bolster between us, Dorothy, so you'll sleep better, and needn't be afraid at all." He did so, and then turned out the light. They undressed silently and climbed into bed. True, through all, to the principles he had learned at his mother's knee he fell off to sleep at once and left her as undisturbed as though he were a candidate for sainthood. ❡ Next day, Dorothy expressed neither gratitude nor vexation until the wind blew her hat off and over a fence. "Never mind, I'll climb over and get it," said Percy. Dorothy, no longer able to keep back the "flapper" in her, let fly: "Do you mean to tell me you could climb over that fence. Why, you couldn't even climb over a bolster!"

421

G REATLY disgruntled because he had been unable to secure the nomination for alderman, Murphy came home and let it out on the missus. "If it hadn't been for you I'd have got it. But they wouldn't give me the nomination because you ain't got no education," he said. ❡ "Is that so," said his spouse, "I held ye back? Well, let me tell ye, if ye'd had paid as much attention to the prayer book as ye did to my bare ass ye'd have been Pope."

422

W HEN the groom returned from the smoking room of the train his bride said to him anxiously: "Have you got our intercourse tickets, Jack?" ❡ "Our what?" he asked. ❡ "Our intercourse tickets," said she. "The conductor will be along directly and you'd better have them ready." ❡ "What are you talking about?" he said. ❡ "Well, I just heard a man in back of us ask, 'where the hell are those fuckin' tickets,'" explained the bride.

423

G OLDBERG's son had just come home from college and the old man asked him what he had learned. "I can't bother now to tell you all I learned," said the son. "But here's a good riddle I picked up: What is it that is hard, and long, and leaks?" ❡ "Bum," said the old man, "to talk to me like that." ❡ "Don't get excited, Pop," said his son. "It's a fountain pen." ❡ "That's a good one," the old man laughed. "Ve'll remember dat." ⟨ The following night at a meeting of his congregation Goldberg sprang the riddle: "What is it that's long, and hard, and it leaks?" The women present raised their hands in horror. The president of the synagogue to make such a riddel as that! Terrible! ⟨ "Don't get nervous, ladies," said Goldberg. "It ain't a prick. It's a fountain pen."

424

THE LOST TURD

A Study in Embarrassment

BILL had not seen his college chum for years. John, tired of the ways of the city had moved into the Canadian Northwest, and had raised a family. Bill determined to visit John, for old time's sake. When he came to the house, far in the woods, it was quite dark. An old man met him, took his horse to the barn, and told him to slip quietly into the attic and go to sleep. ⟨ "Jack'll be more surprised to see you in the morning," the old man said, "and besides you won't be disturbing his sleep, keeping him up late. So you go on upstairs. You'll find a cot there all ready." ⟨ Bill entered the attic on tiptoes. It was quite dark, but he found the cot, and sitting on the edge of it, undressed. When he had got into bed he was seized with a cramp. "I can't redress in time, and I can't rush around looking for a bathroom," he thought. "I guess I'd better lay my load on the floor in a corner, and clean it up in the morning, before Jack sees me." So he dropped a turd carefully in a corner, and went back to bed. But when he rose and looked, the turd was gone! Great was his embarrassment. "Jack has been here and cleaned it up," he said to himself. "I don't know how I'll face him." ❡ But when he met Jack, later, downstairs, his friend made no mention of the turd. Bill was horrified. He at once concluded that Jack's wife had happened into the room, seen the turd, and cleaned it up. But Mrs. Jack, when she was presented to Bill, greeted him so warmly that he knew she could not have been the one. ❡ "Have you met our son, Aleck?" asked Jack, calling him. Bill felt a cold chill run down his spine. He expected to see the child all smeared up with the turd. But a nice, clean, little boy came into the room who seemed so friendly that all of Bill's fears and embarrassments vanished. He did not know how to account for it, but the turd had vanished, and none of these people surely had had a hand in the mysterious disappearance. Greatly relieved as he was, however, he did start when Jack said suddenly, "By the way, have you seen Charlie yet? Here, Charlie, here Charlie," he called, and whistled. Bill turned around. A large turtle was waddling into the room, and on his back was the turd!

425

Two vaudeville actresses were overheard in a theatrical boarding house the other day. "Do you know, Mame," said one, "I went past Edna's bedroom at three o'clock this morning, and her door was open, and she had nothing on but an acrobat!"

426

An IRISHMAN suffering from diarrhea found his bathroom occupied. Without further ado he sat on his rear window sill and pooped down into the yard.

The janitor happened to go out that way at the moment
and a loose turd struck him. Looking up he commenced
to bawl out Pat. ⟨ The latter, however, sneered down
at the Swede. "Ye don't know how lucky ye are," he
shouted. "If I'd a been constipated I'd a broken
yer arm."

427

J ACK had only had his cozy, new car a few days when
he drove into his garage and ordered that it
be re-decorated, and the word "Mayflower" painted,
in elaborate letters, on both sides of the hood. "Don't
be crazy," said his friend, who prided himself on the
soundness of his feeling for the fitness of things, especially in respect to automobiles. "That's a brand-new
Buick, what you want to paint it up like a boat for?"
⟨ "Well, Bill, I'll tell you. I simply got to commemo-
rate. Last night a puritan came across in it."

428

T HERE was a young lady from Exeter,
So pretty that men craned their necks at her,
And one made so brave
As to violently wave
The distinguishing mark of his sex at her.

429

T HE judge looked down on the prisoner with a fierce
frown. The man had committed a heinous crime.
He had been caught in the act of screwing his wife, who
had been dead several hours. ⟨ "Before I pronounce

sentence on you," the judge said, "will you tell me, for my own information, what prompted you to do this deed?" ❡ "Honest, Judge," said the defendant, "I didn't know she as dead. She's been like that for the last twelve years.

430

PETRONIUS: Do you know the reason the arse hole is placed so near the cunt? ❡ Nero: No, why? ❡ Petronius: To discourage men from going down.

431

A MAN dashed into the doctor's office in a great funk. "Look doctor," he screamed, taking out his pecker, "look how red it is, all splotched up. What shall I do for it." ❡ The physician took the tool in his hand a moment, then said, "Get a wet rag and rub it off. Then tell your girl not to use so much lip rouge."

432

AN IRISHWOMAN called to see the doctor and complained that she was almost always in a state of pregnancy. It seems she had tried every known method to prevent conception, but without success. Her husband was a singularly virile fellow, who tore through condoms as if they were tissue paper. Douches had failed again and again, and she wanted the doctor to give her something sure. The physician, who was tired of prescribing for the woman, told her to go home, and whenever she went to bed with Pat to put a two gallon pot over her feet. That, certainly, he said laughing, would prevent further offspring. ❡ To his surprise, however, some months later, she appeared for treatment, pregnant again. "Did you do what I told you?" he demanded sternly. "Sure doctor, and I did," said Bridget. "But mebbe 'twas because I didn't have no two gallon pot, so I used two one-gallon ones, one on each foot."

433

A swell girl was one day picked up by a certain handsome actor, who accompanied her to her apartment. There, with scant formality, she undressed and the actor screwed her. When they were dressing again, he said to her, as a matter of courtesy, "Isn't there anything I can do for you? Do you need some money?" ❡ "Why no," said the girl. "When I like a man I don't take money from him. But, if you have a pocket knife you might leave me that as a souvenir." The actor gladly gave her his knife. She tossed it into a drawer which he noticed was almost filled with knives of all descriptions. ❡ "That's a strange passion," said the actor. "Would you mind telling me why you collect knives, of all things." "Well, you know," said the girl, "right now I'm young and not bad to look at. But I'm providing for the future. When I get old and none of my friends will want to give me a tumble I'll still have these knives. And you know what a boy'll do for a penknife."

434

Two girl friends went to a Turkish bath on ladies' night. One had shaved off the hair around her private parts, and the other commented on it. "How is it that I've got such a bush and you ain't got any hair there?" ❡ "Huh," said her friend, "did you ever see grass grow on a busy street?"

435

ONE of the bunch had told an obviously wild tale. ❡ "Ye've been kissing the blarney stone," said Eddie. ❡ "Kissing it! Hell, he's gone down on it," said Jack.

436

LITTLE Tommy Tripper,
  Naughty little nipper,
He filled his ass
With broken glass
And circumcised the skipper.

437

A FAT man was in a Turkish bath with some of his friends, who were ridiculing him because of his obesity. "Hell, I'll bet it's years since you've seen your pecker," one said to him. "Why don't you diet?" "Dye it, dye it?" he said in bewilderment. "Why, what color is it now?"

438

"WHAT are you looking so sad about?" asked the madam as one of her patrons came downstairs. "Nothing," said the man, "just an accident. I was told by my doctor that I'd go blind if I didn't have three drops of urine put in each eye every day. I got Mamie upstairs and told her to piss three drops into my right eye. She did. But when I said 'shift' she misunderstood me."

439

A TRAVELLING man picked up an Indian woman off a reservation and persuaded her, with the aid of a silver dollar and an imitation diamond ring to lay for him. All during the screw the squaw kept crying, "Wahoo. Wahoo. Wahoo." The drummer could not make out what she meant, and as her English was a strange garble, or gargle if you will, he gave up trying to find out. ℂ Next night he was in a pool room, where a couple of young bucks were engaged in a tense cue duel. One of them made a difficult shot to a side pocket, but the other shouted, "Wahoo." ℂ "I beg your pardon," said the salesman to the Indian, "but did I hear you say 'wahoo'? What does it mean?" ℂ "Wahoo means wrong hole, mister," said the buck.

440

O SCAR WILDE in his search for a bedmate approached a cockney youth in the slums of London and asked him to come to his room with him. "All right, guv'ner," said the cockney. "But before we goes I wants ter know 'oo does it to 'oo and 'oo pyes?"

441

" A H, did I have a party yesterday!" said Meyer to Mose. ℂ "Yeh? What did you do?" ℂ "I went with a girl to her apartment and we both got undressed. Then we had a drink, and I kissed her on the lips." ❡ "Yeh, yeh, go on." ❡ "Then we had another drink, and I kissed her on the nipples." ❡ "Go on, go on." ❡ "We had one more drink, and I kissed her on the navel." ❡ "Yeh, yeh, go ahead, what then . . ." ❡ "Oh, boy, was I drunk!"

442

A CHAP was rattling along a country road in his flivver when he overtook a girl who was crying. He stopped and asked if he could help her. "Yes," she said, "please give me a lift. I was in a Packard with a man, and he tried to make me do something, and I wouldn't, and he told me to get out and walk." ❡ "All right, jump in," said the stranger. The girl sat in the rear seat, and the car bumped and jerked along. Finally she could stand it no longer, and, leaning over, tapped her benefactor on the shoulder. "I'm sorry, but you'll have to let me out," she said. "I'd rather be raped in a Packard than jerked off in a Ford."

443

THE country preacher had announced as his text: "Adultery." Expanding on the subject he vehemently arraigned those brethren who made it a practice to call on the wives of their friends and neighbors for the purpose of giving them physical solace. In the middle of his address one worshipper rose suddenly and made down the aisle. "Where are you going?" the minister asked him. "I just remembered where I left my umbrella," the brother said, continuing on his hasty way.

444

THE young porter in *The Globe* press rooms got married and the boys each contributed something. Besides money some of them brought pieces of furniture to help the youth fix up a home. The foreman gave him a brand new bedspring and mattress. A few days later the porter returned the spring. "Why, what's the matter with it," the foreman asked. "Nothin' boss," said the fellow, "only it feeds too fast."

445

A STORY that deservedly takes its place with the hoary antiquities is the one about the cockney who said to a visiting American in an awe-stricken voice, " 'Ere comes the Queen." "Fuck her," said the American shortly. "Why you can't even approach 'er," said the cockney.

446

A COUPLE of young girls stopped in front of a fruit stand and asked the Italian how much the bananas cost. "Fi' cents each, three for ten," he said. "Dear, ain't they?" commented one. "Oh, well, 'sall right, give us three. We can always eat the other one."

447

TWO girls sitting opposite a man in a trolley began to giggle when they noticed the fly of his trousers was open. "Mister," said one, "your vanity case is open." ¶ "My what?" asked he. ¶ "Your vanity case. Better close it before your lip stick drops out."

448

LITTLE MABEL was visiting her country cousin. As they were walking in the fields Mabel asked her cousin to show her the toilet, so she could 'go pee-pee.' The other girl directed her to the out-house. Mabel took one look inside, and backed away. "That ain't no privy," she said, "that's a fireless cooker."

449

A GROUP of travelling men seated in the smoker of a train approaching New York was joined by a drummer who said, "Well, I've just shot off a wire telling my wife I'll be home in an hour, and she'll have a fine meal on the table all ready for me." ❡ "I don't have to give mine that much notice," said one of the group. "I just call her up from the station, and by the time I get home she's all ready." ❡ "Huh," sneered another of the group. "The first thing I do when I get off the train is to buy a good baseball bat. Then I go home and ring the front bell. I run around to the back door quick, and I haven't missed a son-of-a-bitch in ten trips."

450

DURING the Civil War a soldier accosted a young woman in Mississippi and asked her to accommodate him. "Are you from the 6th Ohio?" she asked. "No," said the soldier. "Or the 12th Massachusetts?" "No." "Or the 69th New York?" "No." "Then I'm sorry," said the woman, "but I can't do nothing for you. I'm kept private for those regiments."

451

Durıng recess one of the boys wrote in large letters on the school wall: "Willie Jones has the biggest prick in school." Miss Smith, the teacher saw this, and in great indignation ordered Willie to remain after class. The rest of the gang waited outside for him. It was an hour before he appeared. ❡ "What'd she do to you?" they demanded. "Did she hit ya? Or what?" ❡ Willie winked upon them. "It pays to advertise," was all he said.

452

Pat was excessively profane over the telephone and the girls had made many complaints against him. One day, exasperated over a succession of wrong numbers, he began to cuss out the girl. "Stop that," she said, "or I'll have to have your phone removed." ❡ "Oh, stick it up your ass," said Pat. Next day two men came from the company, and were about to take away the instrument, when Pat asked if he could square matters by apologizing to the girl. They said he could, and he took down the receiver. ❡ "Girlie," he said, "I'm sorry. You know what I said yesterday, you could stick the phone up your ass?" ❡ "Yes," said she icily. ❡ "Well," floundered Pat, "there's two men to take it out."

453

Jones, while on a drunk, picked up a Swedish girl, and, taking her into a hallway, gave her a standing screw. When he had finished he searched in his pockets to pay the girl, and discovered to his horror that he had only a thin dime. He was very sorry, for he was really not the sort of chap to bilk a girl. So he apologized. "Sorry, girlie," he said, "all I got is a dime." ❡ The girl hesitated a moment, then said, "Ay bane sorry too. Ay bane got no change."

454

THREE fellows were brought before a judge for minor offenses. The magistrate asked one how he felt. "I feel very bad, sir," said he. "Thirty days to feel better in," said the judge. "I feel fine," said the second. "Sixty days," said the judge, "to think over what you have done." "I feel just like a bride on her first night," said the third chap. "How is that?" asked the judge. "I know I'm gonna get it, but I don' know how long it'll be!"

455

THE new stenographer was a terrible grouch. Nobody could ask her to do anything without getting a snappy answer back. She growled at this, grumbled at that, and made herself generally unpleasant. But since she was a good worker the boss let it go at that. ❡ One morning, however, she came in all smiles. She hummed to herself as she rattled the keys, and answered pleasantly when she was spoken to. Everybody was amazed. The boss gave her a lot of correspondence to answer. She did it in jig time, and laid the letters on his desk for him to sign. Mystified, he looked at her. ❡ "What's the matter, Mame?" he said, "Are you sick?" ❡ She grinned back at him. "I'll tell the world I am!"

456

"How did you get that black eye?" ❡ "I was calling on a gal last night, and we were in her parlor, dancing, while the victrola was playing, and her old man came in, and the bastard is deaf."

457

A DISTINGUISHED critic is fond of telling the story of the man who registered at a Swiss hotel and was put in the same room with the strong man from a circus. The late-comer found Hercules undressed in the room, taking his exercise. A parade passed at the moment and the strong man leaned out of the window to watch it pass. The other, being of a sodomistic turn of mind, could not resist the fair target that presented itself, and rammed his pecker home. The strong man turned his head, straightened himself, and, contracting his anal cheeks, roared, "Oho, so that's it. Come with me!" and led his man by the pecker to the lock-up.

458

A T THE same hotel another sodomist registered and was assigned to a room which already had an occupant. The clerk, who knew the registrant, tipped him off that the early arrival was not averse to a bout, but that for form's sake he might put up a struggle. "But don't you pay any attention to him. You go ahead, he likes it," said the clerk. ❡ Next morning the sodomist came down and the clerk asked him how he had fared. ❡ "It was quite easy," he answered. "He put up no struggle at all." ❡ "My God," said the clerk,

"I put you in the wrong room. That was the archbishop."

459

A YOUTH entered a drugstore jubilantly. "Boss," he said, "I'm getting married tonight. So gimme ten cents worth of vaseline." Next day he came in, contritely. "Pardon me, boss," he hesitated, "but could you change that vaseline for me to alum?"

460

AN AMERICAN who was attending a banquet in a London house, given by Lady Brighton, felt quite embarrassed when the lady broke wind. One of the Englishmen rose immediately, said, "I beg your pardon," and sat down again. Once more the lady farted and another English guest rose and apologized. ❡ "What's the idea?" asked the American of his neighbor. ❡ "Why don't you know? That's the gentlemanly thing to do," said the other. ❡ Again her ladyship let go, but this time the American rose, restraining another Englishman who was about to get up. "I beg your pardon, sir," he said, "but this one is on me."

461

RUPERT was in court, waiting his turn before the bar. He noticed a number of women step up in rapid succession before the judge, say, "I'm a whore," and get off with a five-dollar fine. So when he was called Rupert put in the same plea. "What's that?" demanded the jury. "Yessir," said Rupert, "I'm a fairy whore." "Here," said the judge to the attendant, "take this man in the next room and see whether what he says is true." The attendant returned in a couple of minutes and said, "Whore nothin', yer honor. The fella has a pecker nine inches long." "Ninety days," roared the judge. But Rupert only laughed. "If I'd had a hard on, judge, I reckon yuh'd given me life," he chuckled.

462

M ARIE had come home late and her mother demanded an explanation. "I was out with Randal," said her daughter. "We were by the railroad tracks, foolin' around. He didn't do nothin', maw. He just maybe got about a half inch in." "You be careful," said her mother. "Don't trifle with that fellow." Next night, Marie came in late again, with the same explanation, except that this time her friend had penetrated about an inch and a half. Succeeding nights further progress was reported, till she told her mother one night that her gentlemen friend had put in about, er, nine inches. "You be careful, Marie," her mother admonished, "or that feller'll rape you!"

463

S EEING how successful Nick, his Greek friend, was with *Say it With Flowers*, Tony who had a fruit stand, adapted it to the trenchant *Do it With Bananas*.

464

P ERKINS was a guest at a fine English home where the amusement of the moment was asking riddles and making charades. When it came his turn he asked,

"What is it that's round, and hot, and moist, and covered with hair?" ❡ Horrified, the others gave it up. ❡ "It's a cunt," Perkins said simply. ❡ "James, give the man his hat and coat," said the hostess, sternly. Perkins, in disgrace, went to the colonies. Years later he returned to England, rich and respected. Again he was invited to the fine home, and again he asked his riddle. Everybody smiled this time, and waited for the brilliant answer they were certain would come. ❡ "What is it that's round, and hot, and moist, and covered with hair?" he repeated. All gave up. ❡ "My hat and coat, James," said Perkins. "It's still a cunt."

465

BUGS BAER, looking at a poster of a *Follies'* girl dressed in negligee of silk said, with a sneer: "Huh, she never farted through silk all her life."

466

A DEAF-MUTE was witness in a rape case. It was almost certain from former evidence that this fellow had watched the girl go into the barn, had seen the man follow her, and had witnessed the rape. Under written cross-examination this evidence was confirmed in the following manner: ❡ "You say you saw the girl walk into the barn?" the attorney began. Here the deaf-mute held two fingers close together on the desk and made them walk with mincing steps. ❡ "You say the man followed her into the barn?" Here the deaf-mute made the two fingers stride. "You have told us that they remained some time in the barn, and that the girl came out first walking slowly. Is that correct?" The witness nodded affirmatively, and held his fingers wide apart making them walk with wide steps. "And the man followed, more slowly?" The fingers made stumbling movements of walking. Then the deaf-mute, gurgling and pointing excitedly to himself, made two fingers walk with the middle finger sticking up, rigid. ℂ The girl was pronounced raped.

467

A woman who kept a Chinese servant was considerably annoyed by his failure to knock on the door before entering a room. Several times he had urbanely come into her boudoir, while she was totally undressed. So she spoke to him about it. "Don't come into my bedroom hereafter," she said, "without knocking. I may not be dressed and I don't want to be embarrassed." ℂ Charley smiled a bland acquiescence. Never again did it happen. But Charley never knocked on the door. Wondering how he could do it, the madame asked him. "Velly simple," said Charley. "Beflore me come in, me look thlough keyhole. If no dlessed, me no come in."

468

"What a life," said one flee to another the other day. "I fell asleep on a cunt and I wake up on a moustache."

469

Prix: Why is it so many young girls who marry old men leave them? Bollix: Very easy. They prefer hot dog to cold tongue.

470

TEACHER had asked her pupils to make rhyming verses of two lines each. Many elegant specimins were submitted, until little Johnny rose and offered:
"May Jane McKane, of Boston, Mass.
Went into the water up to her ankle."
❡ "Why that doesn't rhyme," said the teacher. ❡ "It will," said Johnny, "when the tide comes in."

471

IT was said of a certain notorious 'cunnilinge', or 'browning', as the current tongue has it, that he was operated on for appendicitis and a hair mattress was taken out.

472

THE most perilous indoor sport is said to be:
BUTTON, BUTTON, HERE COMES MY HUSBAND.

473

"SEND me the book-keeper," roared the senior partner. And when that worthy appeared he bawled him out properly. "I can't stand for much more of this," he said. "Last year you forged two checks in my name. Two weeks ago I found out you were giving away our business secrets, and last night I heard you've been screwing my daughter. The next least little thing you do, — out you go."

474

THE baroness lay in the agony of death. Having called her husband to her side she said: "Armand, what I am about to say will surprise you, but I cannot die without this confession. I have deceived you with the butler." ❦ The baron looked down on her coldly. "My dear," he said, "why do you suppose I gave you the poison?"

475

Cuddy: What's a good name for Brooklyn baby carriages? ❦ Clitoris: Blunderbusses.

476

"My boy is quite a slicker," said old Silas to a crony. "Since he got out of school he's been hellin' around with a burlesque queen. I heard he was in bed with her all last night. I believe if he'd played his cards right he might 'a screwed her."

477

A certain actor complained to a friend in the Green Room Club that he seemed always to be cast for unsympathetic roles. "In the last four shows I've played a son-of-a-bitch bastard." ❦ "Too bad," sympathized a friend. "It's this type-casting that's ruining the American stage."

478

Fred came up to town all set for adventure. He called up a girl whose number a friend had given him, and made a date for a musical show. They were installed in seats on the front row at the Shubert, right over by one of those wise drummers when Fred began his attack. "Since you say you pose for artists I want you to tell me something I've always wanted to know about models." ❦ "What's that?" ❦ "Why it's whether they shave it off down there." ❦ The drummer, whose eyes had been fastened on the open legs of this girl, now pricked up his ears. ❦ "Of course we all shave there," she replied casually. "No model can get a job unless she does that." ❦ The wise drummer: "Say, girlie, you haven't posed in a long while, have you?"

479

THERE was a young man from Cape Corn,
    Who wished that he never was born,
He wouldn't have been,
But the rubber was thin,
    And neither one knew it was torn.

480

THE power of advertising is often demonstrated in other ways than by the records of increased sales. So various are the activities of the *Purity Leagues* in this country, however, that those who are addicted to this habit must be very careful how they word their ads or they may be arraigned for obscenity. This is well illustrated by the following episode which shows how impure associations can be read into even the most innocent arrangement of words. ❦ Pearl Mirandy, a well-made negress, had been impressed by the poster which reads, "USE VELOX PAPER." Now Pearl had a tender bum, and was continually experimenting with various toilet papers. Having determined to make a trial of the above-mentioned article, she approached a drugstore clerk for it. "What have you?" the genial fel-

low asked, "a large Brownie, or . . ." "See here, young man,
don't you git personal. I didn't come in here to be insulted."

481

THERE was a young man from Florida
    Got stuck on a nasty, old, horrid whore.
When he got into bed
He said, "God strike me dead,
    This ain't a cunt, it's a corridor."

482

PRIX: Why is a sailor's pants like a small hotel.
    Bollix: Very easy. There's no ball room.

483

ONE of those benign lady settlement workers stopped
a hard-looking youngster and asked where his
father was. ❡ "Ain't got no father," said the kid.
❡ "And your mother?" ❡ "Ain't got no mother."
❡ "Ah, too bad. When did she pass away?" ❡ "I never
had no mother." ❡ "Then how were you born?"
the lady settlement worker asked in dulcet tones.
❡ "Some damn guerilla knocked up my aunt!"

484

THERE can be little doubt the last depth possible to
masculine *naïveté* has been sounded in the following tale. ❡ It was the wedding night of the only son
of a most proper family in Brookline. Of the body of
woman he only knew vaguely that the place between
her legs was some sort of objective. This suspicion

was confirmed at their first encounter when he learned
this region is topped by a tuft of hair. When his new-
made bride rose and raised her arms to arrange her
hair for the night he noticed two similar tufts of hair
in her armpits. ⟨ "Oh gee," he exclaimed, "just to
think there are two more places still."

485

"MY goodness," said one flapper to another at a
country club. "See that Myrtle girl swim!
Ain't she the cat's — " ⟨ "Why shouldn't she be a
great swimmer?" said her friend. "Ain't you heard
she used to be a streetwalker in Venice?"

486

THE following titles are suggested as collateral
reading of especially pertinent significance to
American students:

The Great Rubber Failure	Iva Child.
A Girl's Anxiety	R. U. Cumming.
(Also attributed to	Mr. Period.)
Shepherd's Delight	A. Ramsbottom.
The Shiek's Demand	Musthapha Boy.
Hubby's Delight	Mike Hunt.
At the Twelvth Time	John Henry Bent.
The Contented Wife	John Thomas Everhard.
The Dawn of Love	Holden Hizcock.
The Easiest Way	Eileen Back.
The Hungry Lover	E. Nawder Titsoff.
The Optional Route	R. Sole.
Limitation of Offspring	Dr. Kutcha Kockoff.
The Happy Honeymoon	Maud Fitzgerald and Gerald Fitzmaud.

487

From here, doctor? .. Seein' as 'ow you've got a load of cunt aboard I won't sye nothin' nawsty, all I sye is my bloody arse'ole to you, you bloomin' fuck . . . You, Prussian vomit . . . Hope you're feeling better . . . anybody got a daily paper? wait, get a bunch of fresh grass . . . Shit, I don't wanna dance, mamma, when I dance I sweat and when I sweat I stink and when I stink the boys don't like me. . . . What's the most beautiful part of a woman? There has been general unanimity, except that some have spelled with a k . . . IMMORTALITY . . . Immorality, the station house, look through keyhole you'll see . . . kiss my ass I'm going. Sit down, you cocksucker, sit down . . . Silver dollar Mary, a silver dollar with a hole in it that big is worth only half. You put your foot in it, no, but I coul . . . she's your sister, he ain't your father . . . Lord and Lady 'Awkins put wax in rats' holes . . . is soles, are soles, 'oos vulgar neaow . . . A pedlar goes around town ballin' out his wares . . . As good fish in the sea as ever were caught. I hate to lose fish after I have hook in him maybe saxteen, saventeen times . . . Strapped dick to leg, quick, doctor, can't get let down . . . Gonna cut off his bonus . . . Mandy goin' to get married, didn't even know she was preg . . . Hey, join Ku Klux, I'm a wizard under de sheets . . . I'm always a Goblin under de sheets . . . If anybody guesses the right answer I'll put out the lights.*

488

It's a long lane that has no roadhouse.

* It is hardly necessary to point out the remarkable similarity of this anecdote to certain episodes in the work of James Joyce.

489

A SAILOR met with a whore on the Commons. The sea-man was widely-traveled, and the whore was not only widely-read, she was erudite. He had struck up a conversation with her because she carried under her arm a copy of that curious and informative eastern manual of erotics, the *Kama Sutra of Vatsyayana*. He, having spent much time in the Far East, was acquainted with it as well as with the *Ananga Ranga* and the *Perfumed Garden*. As they sat on a bench discussing the ancient sexual lore in these rare books, he became aware of a strangely pungent odor which he soon realized came from her mouth. "Hum," he breathed ecstatically, "like a breath from the Orient!" ❮ "Well, it ought to be," she replied casually. "I just had a fellatio session with a Chinaman."

490

DURING the rage for cross-word puzzles with which some enterprising business man lately succeeded in infecting almost the entire adult as well as infant population of this country, a very proper middle-aged woman went about asking this question: "What is a word of six letters that is the name of a four-legged animal that has whiskers and is bald?" ❮ It should be explained that this lady prided herself on the nice choice of her acquaintances, and that if any one in her presence touched, even in a philosophical or scientific manner, on subjects not to her prejudices orthodox he was promptly stricken from the circle of her elect as a corrupting influence and a degenerate. It should also be explained that her suppressions were due not so much to hypocrisy inherent in her as to the influence of an aged husband, — not, however, so aged as ignorant and hypocritical. ⦅ After your futile attempts to help her identify this strange animal she would obtain her release by ejaculating innocently, "A tomcat, of course!"

491

Henry took his bride to Florida on their honeymoon trip and in one brief week had succeeded in awakening in the apt girl a deep appreciation of conjugal pleasures. Then they met an old maid who was so impressed by the evident potency of this young man she made a proposal that Henry, who was a hardworking film salesman, felt he could not refuse. The only trouble was, would May consent. ⦅ "Honey," he explained, "the old girl's going to be our salvation. She's saved eighty thousand dollars to buy a swell mausoleum to be buried in. But she wants to taste once of the flesh before she dies, and she's offered me ten thousand of it if I'll spend one night with her. Don't you think you can spare me for one night? Think what it'll mean to us." ⦅ Very reluctantly May consented. But two days passed, and no Henry; four days, six days, and no Henry. On the eighth day, when her patience had been tried to the breaking point, in came Henry jubilantly waving an eighty thousand dollar wad of bills. ⦅ "Look, honsie, the old girl decided she'd make a week of it and be buried in the potters' field!"

492

Prix: What is the most useless space in the world?
Bollix: Very easy. The space between twin beds.

493

Here lies the body of Mary May Charlotte,
  Born a virgin, died a harlot;
For 18 yrs. she kept her virginity,
A damn long time for this vicinity.

494

Mrs. Leech, the proprietor of a large whorehouse in Chicgao, needed a loan of three thousand dollars. She desired to make some improvemens on her already elaborate establishment, improvements which were to contribute to the convenience and comfort of her guests since they were necessary to greater efficiency and higher profits. ❡ But when she approached her banker for the money he hesitated. Whereupon she delivered an harangue to the effect that he knew as well as she that her credit was as good as that of anybody he had on his books, and that just because she employed all female labor was no reason why her money — etcetera, etcetera. Her tongue won the day, and the banker asked her on what terms she would make re-payment. "I'll pay you the first thousand at the end of thirty days, the second thousand at the end of sixty, and the third at the end of ninety." ❡ "That's all right, Mrs. Leech. But I thought you needed the money longer. As long as we're granting the loan we can give you more time. Only don't pledge yourself to what you may not be able to do." ❡ "Sure I can do it. Don't we have the Elks' convention in three weeks, the Odd Fellows' next month, and the Shriners' the month after?" ❡ So the loan was arranged, and madame made her repairs.

But at the end of thirty days she came in with the entire three thousand dollars. "Why, Mrs. Leech," said the banker, "you have time. How does it happen you bring it all in so soon?" ⟨ "You know, Billy, I plum forgot this was the month of the Eucharist congress."

495

MINNIE, a hillbilly gal in good ol' Kentucky, had tended her little patch of cabbages carefully all Summer. One evening, Zandie, her mule, got into the garden and made great havoc before Minnie saw him from the kitchen. She ran out all a-flutter motioning wildly and crying, "Shoo, shoo, here, you ol' mule. Git away from there, you good fer nothin'." Homer Mose, looking on from the next yard saw how she was lifting her skirts high and letting them fall in the manner peculiar to such women when they would frighten off an animal. But Zandie continued to feed, good-naturedly swinging his tool. "Look out, Minnie," Mose called; "first thing you know that mule'll think you-all wants to put a collar on him."

496

SAM and Marie had come home from a party where she had quarreled violently with him because he had danced with an old friend of whom she was jealous. If there had been an extra sofa in the house she certainly would not have gone to bed with him that night. As it was she was compelled to sleep with him or on the floor. Sam, who was of a placid disposition, was not at all troubled, and drew up his legs at once for sleep. "Get your damn knee off my back," she yelled suddenly. "That's not my knee, honey," said Sam. ⟨ After a moment Marie ventured plaintively, "Too bad we quarreled, isn't it, Sammy?" "It's a damn shame," he said carelessly, and turned over for sleep. ⟨ (Of course it was his knee all the time.)

497

Two old fellows were comparing the ravages time had made in their sexual powers when one burst out: "Hell, Bill, it takes me all night to do now what I used to do all night."

498

It was down in good old North Carolina and Sam Johnson's mules were stalling square on a railroad track. Sammy whipped them under the forelocks. "Go 'long there Jake. Git 'long Maud. You're sure lazy, you ol' mule." One wondered which to admire most, the stubbornness of the mules or the patience of Sam. He had been beating them and cursing them to no purpose a full hour when a train whistled. "Lordy," cried Sam, "here comes the ten-forty. Git 'long now, mule. You'll sure move when that engine hits you." True to southern tradition the Charleston Limited was ambling along at about twenty miles an hour. The engineer saw the fella's predicament in time to stop his train. He crawled down and came up to the scene. "Can't git em to move, man. They're stuck. An' when my mule's stuck I might as well take a day off." "Well, let me see what I can do with them," said the engineer. "Give me the reins." He then gave one of the beasts a great kick in the belly. The hillside resounded with a prolonged and prodigious fart, (I beg your pardon, but there is really no other word that quite expresses the fact). He did the same to the other mule, and there was another equally impressive bombardment of asinine intestinal gas. Whereupon they moved on as though automatically. "Well," said the placid Sam, "you railroad fellows seem to know all about makin' things go. But how wuz I to know they had the airbrakes on?"

499

IT was a bright day in heaven. But the old amusement park, which enjoyed no longer the vogue of former days, was quiet as a tomb. Tastes had changed. Business was so slack St. Peter was dozing at the gate when God came along on a tour of inspection. He was spreading an aura of gloom so deep it woke Peter out of his sweet dreams. ❡ "Hell, papa," he advised, "why don't you leave all your worries and go down to earth again for one of those good old times?" ❡ "No, Peter, no more of that for me. I knocked up a Jewish girl some two thousand years ago, and they haven't done talking about it yet."

500

WELL, if Eve had only liked bananas better we'd all still be in Paradise.

INDEX

MORE GOOD DIRTY JOKES

MORE GOOD DIRTY JOKES

MORE GOOD DIRTY JOKES

MORE GOOD DIRTY JOKES

MORE GOOD DIRTY JOKES

MORE GOOD DIRTY JOKES